# Critical Thinking for Psychology

# BPS Student Guides

*BPS Student Guides* are short, accessible texts on key skills or the core elements of a degree, designed with the needs of students in mind.

# Critical Thinking for Psychology

## A Student Guide

**MARK FORSHAW**

*Library of Congress Cataloging-in-Publication Data*

Forshaw, Mark.
    Critical thinking for psychology : a student guide / Mark Forshaw.
        p.   cm.
    Includes bibliographical references and index.
    ISBN 978-1-4051-9118-0 (hardback)—ISBN 978-1-4051-9117-3 (pbk.)
        1. Critical thinking.   2. Psychology.   I. Title.
    BF441.F66   2012
    153.4'2—dc23

                                                2012004753

A catalogue record for this book is available from the British Library

Set in 12/13.5pt Dante MT by MPS Limited, Chennai, India
Printed in Great Britain by TJ International, Padstow, Cornwall

The British Psychological Society's free Research Digest e-mail service rounds up the latest research and relates it to your syllabus in a user-friendly way. To subscribe go to www.researchdigest.org.uk or send a blank e-mail to subscribe-rd@lists.bps.org.uk.

Senior Commissioning Editor:        Andrew McAleer
Assistant Editor:                   Katharine Earwaker
Marketing Managers:                 Fran Hunt and Jo Underwood
Project Editor:                     Juliet Booker

DEDICATED TO
THE MEMORY OF MY FATHER, KEVIN JOHN FORSHAW

This book is about critical thinking applied to psychology. In order to do just that, I have to take you on a journey somewhat, into other areas first. I begin with talking about critical thinking as applied to everyday life, and then I concentrate more on psychology.

I wrote this book mainly in order to help students understand what is meant by critical thinking in an academic context. The key reason for this is because student feedback frequently features comments about critical thinking, but often those students receiving it don't actually know what it means. Lecturers sometimes find it difficult to explain, because to do so involves giving lots of examples, and it would take a long time to go into enough detail to be useful. Therefore, a book on that very subject, written for psychology students, gets us around that problem, I hope.

The book is intended to be read from start to finish, because the arguments you find in here develop as you work through. If you dip into it, you might not get the best from the book, even though it is possible to read it that way.

*Dr Mark Forshaw*

I am grateful to Andrew McAleer at Wiley Blackwell for our invaluable, long-established, convivial working relationship, and, on this project in particular, for his understanding when I took uncharacteristically long to write this book. Thanks to my colleague, Anja Rutten, for some very helpful suggestions, and to Laura Fletcher, my valuable illustrator. I am also grateful to the three reviewers who commented on the first draft and who will find that I took many of their suggestions on board. As always, I thank Amanda Crowfoot, on this occasion for convincing me that travelling the world is a good idea. The more you experience, the better you understand things. The better you understand things, the more critical your thinking. For more than 21 years, she has provided a crucial second perspective on everything. I cannot imagine how stupid I would be now without that.

# 1 Getting Started on Critical Thinking

## WHAT IS CRITICAL THINKING?

As you would imagine, definitions of critical thinking vary from author to author, but there are certain key features that we can draw out. While there are debates about what constitutes *good* critical thinking, there are a few facts we can start with.

Usually critical thinking involves the production of an **argument** *about an argument*. The first speaker or writer says something, and the critic examines the argument of the first speaker, providing counterarguments that undermine the original proposition. It can be quite a controversial area – arguments can become quite personal and aggressive – but remember when you are trying to think critically yourself to stay calm, no matter how ridiculous what you've been presented with is. Construct your counterargument logically, methodically, slowly, and maintain a good pace. Rarely does anyone assume that someone who is shouting, ranting or excited is making a good point: we tend to listen to calm people much more. Shouting gets you noticed, but it doesn't get you agreed with. It's always useful to think about the argument someone is making in the context of the tone of their speech, and any particular reasons they might have for making the comments they are making. What are the motives of the person making claims? What is their agenda? A politician, a parent, a feminist, a patient or a film critic all have things they want to achieve, and what they say might be influenced by those wider aims; they don't exist in a vacuum. Similarly, what is the quality of the information that you are being provided with in an argument? Can you trust its source? Just because someone has found a 'fact' on the internet or even in a book does not mean that it is indisputable. Always check so-called facts that are presented to you. We'll discuss these issues again later in the book.

Critical thinking is, most of the time, closely related to critical reading. After all, when we ask students to think critically, and mark down their work because it doesn't show critical thinking, what we really mean is that they have not demonstrated that they read original sources critically.

Critical thinking is largely associated with an argument. This involves putting forward *positions*, which further the argument as we read or speak on it. In common parlance, we refer to two people disagreeing as 'having an argument', as if these were synonymous. However, unless new positions are being generated, they are not actually arguing, but disagreeing. An example of a disagreement is to be found in traditional pantomime:

> *'He's behind you!'*
> *'Oh, no he isn't!'*
> *'Oh, yes he is!'*
> *'Oh, no he isn't!'*
> *'Oh, yes he is!'*

All that is happening is that both parties are repeating a single position: nothing develops. It's a disagreement, not an argument. When we think critically, we have to do so by first assessing what someone's position is, then providing a critique of their argument to support that position.

## Defining critical thinking

It might be useful to examine some common or 'classic' definitions of critical thinking.

John Dewey is regarded as the modern reviver of critical thinking philosophy, although he called it, interestingly enough, 'reflective thinking'. He said it was the:

---

Active, persistent, and careful consideration of a belief or supposed form of knowledge in the light of the grounds which support it and the further conclusions to which it tends.

*(Dewey, 1909, p.9)*

---

This seems very much like a common-sense statement rather than something deeper, but if we apply some critical thinking to this definition of critical thinking (perhaps we could call that *metacritical thinking*), we see something more profound emerging. It is clear from this that critical thinking has a method, and that method must be active and persistent. We keep on asking questions until we have no more to ask. We base our enquiries on evidence ('the grounds which support it'), and we have an eye on the implications and conclusions of any belief (i.e. we think about the uses to which an argument could be put, because sometimes we can predict what others will make of our ideas, and what awful consequences might arise).

Here is one more definition for you, this time from Richard Paul, who is also famous for his use of **Socratic questioning** (see below):

---

Critical thinking is that mode of thinking – about any subject, content or problem – in which the thinker improves the quality of his or her thinking by skilfully taking charge of the structures inherent in thinking and imposing intellectual standards upon them.

*(Paul, Fisher, & Nosich, 1993, p.4)*

---

Here we have clear reference to 'metacritical' thinking and an allusion to the use of method; again we could call that scientific method, if appropriate, as in the case of much of psychology.

It seems, therefore, that critical thinking needs to have some implicit or explicit structure, and by implication, some method. It is for the purpose of improving the quality of thinking, and therefore the production of one's own arguments.

# PSYCHOLOGY AND CRITICAL THINKING

One thing missing from these definitions is the notion of *creative* thinking. For some writers on the subject, it seems as if critical thinking has become divorced from the act of creation. That is probably an unnecessary and dangerous step. Good critical thinking can be creative: it's all about putting ideas together in new ways and making us think of things we didn't think of before. Perhaps these days we make a false distinction between creative people and scientific people, and perhaps we think that critical thinking belongs in the scientific camp. This is faulty thinking. Science is just as creative as the arts, albeit in slightly different ways, and the arts are just as critical as science. Psychology is in a fascinating position, in that it forms the bridge between the two. We can look in either direction for ideas to shape our theories, and psychologists are often trained in the arts, the sciences or both.

When you read this book, think about psychology, what it means to you and where it fits in, and try to keep the bigger picture of what psychology is in your mind. Psychology is a massive subject, and encroaches on sociology, medicine, philosophy and so on. It has a wide range of methods, from the anti-scientific approaches of the critical qualitative researchers through to the biological psychologists, whose methods are indistinguishable from those used by formal scientists. Perhaps, therefore, you will find contradictions within psychology – unless you only view one area of psychology at a time and think about that in relation to issues concerning critical thinking. When people dismiss psychology as 'mumbo jumbo', do they mean all of psychology, or just bits of it? When people champion psychology for its progress and findings, do they mean all of it, or just bits of it?

Tied in with all of this is the argument about whether psychology is a science or an art. It is the bridge between the two, and bridges have foundations on both sides of the river. From now on, as you read, keep asking yourself a slightly different question: is psychology an artful science, or a scientific art? Ask yourself also, at every turn, whether you feel that psychologists are involved in finding things out, or asking more and more questions? Concern yourself with not only the immediate picture – that is, working out whether or not a particular piece of research is valid – but also with the bigger picture, that of where all our evidence is heading. Are we getting somewhere, and if so, in what direction?

## CHAPTER 1 – CRITICAL QUESTIONS

1. What is critical thinking? Can you define it easily, and if not, why not?
2. 'If you want to think critically, knowing what critical thinking is is half the battle': discuss.

# 2 Logic and the Philosophy of Critical Thinking

When we start to venture into the very bases upon which critical thinking is built, we head off into the territory of philosophers and mathematicians. A great deal of critical thinking can be said to be the application of the philosopher's tools to check out which arguments stand up and which don't.

Fundamentally, the philosophy of critical thinking is all about fallacies and truth. It won't help to spend any time on the details of truth as defined in **propositional logic** per se. In propositional logic, truth only refers to something being valid or making sense in its context – it doesn't matter if it is true in the real world. Truth is something that follows from something else, logically, but what it follows from doesn't have to be true in any common-sense way. Be aware of that when you read about 'truth' in philosophy texts – or perhaps I should say *if* you read about truth in philosophy texts.

For this book we will concentrate instead on the common-sense notion of truth and falsehood, since that is what we really need when we are thinking and writing critically about arguments put to us in articles and books. We sometimes do still need to resort to syllogistic reasoning, however (reasoning of the form 'All raccoons are animals, this animal is a raccoon, therefore all animals are raccoons'). In order to tell truth from falsehood, we need to understand the nature of falsehood itself, and that requires us to be familiar with the concept of the *fallacy*. A fallacy is an incorrect conclusion, or a misbelief derived from faulty evidence. Fallacies come in many forms. We will deal with some of the most famous ones here, which crop up time and again, not only in the media, but also in student work – and in some of the work of those who really should know better!

## Non sequitur

**Non sequitur** is derived from the Latin for 'it does not follow'; this is arguably one of the most common fallacies in student writing. Put simply, it is often created by the misuse of 'therefore', 'because' or 'thus'. Examples could be:

- Psychology developed the way it did because of the behaviourists.
- People use their eyes as a gateway to the world, therefore there is no access without seeing.
- Many people resort to stereotyping the unknown, thus creating a society of prejudice.

In each case here, the conclusion simply does not follow the **premise** (i.e. the starting point doesn't logically lead to the end point). Behaviourism did probably help to shape psychology, but not alone. Blind people obviously have access to the world without seeing it, and prejudice is not the inevitable and only consequence of stereotyping.

Some people make a *non sequitur* mistake accidentally, especially students, but you need to be aware of those who deliberately use this in the hope that you'll get sucked in by their weak arguments. Politicians will say things like 'Hard work is good for people, therefore we are cutting benefits to encourage more people into work'.

## Slippery slope

This is exactly what its name implies: the **slippery slope** fallacy involves attempting to strengthen an argument, convince or persuade using the fallacy that something being argued against is the 'thin end of the wedge', or the 'tip of the iceberg'. This is, if you accept A, then B will happen, and it will get worse, causing C and D and so on. Whilst sometimes this is true, such arguments are rarely presented with evidence. Often these arguments are subtly joined with a series of events that are not discussed in terms of their probability. This means that although the arguments are possible and logical, they are not probable. This is where the debate falls down.

Let us take an example. You have probably heard of the example of chaos theory that talks about a butterfly flapping its wings in Brazil and causing a tornado in Texas. At least, that's one version of the idea, which has been knocking around for about a century in various incarnations (it seems that originally it was a seagull, not a butterfly). This 'butterfly effect' is perfectly possible, according to the mathematics of dependent systems, because a tiny flap of the butterfly's wings causes a slight alteration in air patterns, which, if combined with other patterns and yet more weather patterns on a grander scale, leads to global consequences. However, the butterfly doesn't really cause the tornado in any useful or meaningful sense. In fact, this is where it gets really interesting. The original idea behind this poetic image is the point that we can't know certain things, not that we can. So people who use a slippery slope argument are actually arguing against themselves, because they are saying that A could lead to B, C, D, E, etc., whereas the 'evidence' they cite isn't evidence at all. Because there are a lot of butterflies out there, not to mention every other thing in the world that could have an effect on another thing, and another, and so on, we simply can't be sure what led to what. That's the point of the butterfly idea: we can't possibly know what made the tornado in Texas – weather systems are too complicated. It's why we get weather predictions wrong a lot of the time. In fact, while the butterfly in Brazil might be part of a chain of untraceable connections to the tornado in Texas, there's another possibility that is equally as likely. Can you guess what it is? The butterfly is equally likely to have *prevented* the tornado by flapping its wings. How's that for turning an argument on its head?

Another related phenomenon is the **domino effect**, in which one thing directly leads to another, to another, then to another and so on. Then we have the **snowball effect**, in which a small thing grows and grows into something more important or serious. They are all, in popular culture, used in very similar ways, and are all forms of slippery slope argument. Sometimes, there is a genuine slippery slope, but our ability to predict that future slope from any point in time is very weak. We can sometimes see slippery slopes easily with the benefit of hindsight, but not usually in advance. Therefore, when someone uses a slippery slope argument, ask the following questions:

- What is the evidence for the link between A and B, or B and C and so on?
- What is the probability of each 'link' occurring, and what, therefore, is the combined probability of the whole chain occurring?

The last point is the most important. Although the link between A and B might be strong, and also strong between B and C, and C and D, it doesn't mean that the likelihood of the whole chain of events happening is particularly high. Mathematicians also consider whether the events in the chain are related to each other or independent at each point. This makes a big difference to the probability of the chain. When the events are independent, we have something called a **Markov chain**. There is a known probability that A will lead to B, or perhaps to something else instead. There is a known probability that B will lead to C, and so on. This is a Markov chain, allowing us to work out the final probability that A will lead to D, or even Z. Each step isn't dependent on the previous steps. However, most real-world probabilities are not like this, because what happened before often influences the chances of certain things happening next. We learn from history. If we didn't, everything would be calculable using Markov chains.

## *Tu quoque*

Most fallacies have Latin names in addition to English ones, and I have chosen to give you the Latin here. **Tu quoque** translates, roughly, as 'you too'. If someone accuses you of something, you can suggest that they have done the same thing themselves. This is the essence of the argument.

> '*I think you are being disingenuous.*'
> '*You were disingenuous yourself last week!*'

The reasoning is flawed. Just because I have done something does not mean that you are excused from it yourself. Although it might imply some hypocrisy, that is in fact irrelevant to the argument.

Imagine a fat chain-smoking alcoholic doctor. Now imagine your reaction when he tells you to lose weight, give up smoking, and cut down on your drinking. You might get angry, and say 'Who are you to tell me that?' Of course, if you think about it for a moment, that reaction makes no sense other than emotionally. It truly doesn't matter what the doctor does. He is qualified in medicine, and is giving you facts about the harm caused by being overweight, smoking cigarettes and drinking too much. Those facts do not change in relation to his own behaviour. If doctors all smoked, smoking would not become less dangerous. Put that way, your reaction would be ridiculous. I'm not saying it isn't understandable, since we're all human beings, but critical thinking means standing outside of your emotional reactions to things and seeing them for what they really are. It also means that it is important to remain calm when *presenting* your ideas and arguments to other people.

## Post hoc ergo propter hoc

The **post hoc ergo propter hoc** argument is something that all psychologists are very familiar with. It is the argument that because two things happen together, one causes the other. In fact, we are taught very firmly that this is not the case – that is, that correlation does not mean causation. What psychologists aren't normally taught is the distinction between necessary and sufficient conditions, and I think it is useful for us to discuss those here.

A necessary condition is one in which, if B happens, A must have been present. However, A being present doesn't mean that B will happen. When it is cold, it snows. It isn't even particularly warm when there's snow on the ground. So, if snow happens, it is cold. But cold weather doesn't mean it will always snow.

A sufficient condition is one in which A being present does mean that B will happen, but that something else might have caused B. That is, B can occur without A, but when you have A, you'll always expect B. For example, a joke makes people smile, but you can smile without a joke being told. If a joke is told, a smile is almost certainly likely, but is not the only reason for smiles to occur.

## *Argument from ignorance*

Put simply, **argument from ignorance** (*argumentum ad ignorantiam*) means assuming that unless something has been proved to be false, it must be true. Freud's main premises are based on this. It is probably impossible to prove Freud incorrect, and this leads some to claim that Freud cannot be wrong. It's very difficult to get anywhere with someone using this kind of argument, because it is fundamentally illogical, but the very fact that the person uses it demonstrates a certain lack in their understanding of logic, which might prevent them from seeing your point! If you claim that the moon is made of cheese, then that doesn't make it true until you've disproved it. If this were the case, we could live our lives by all sorts of incredible ideas that can't easily be proved false. For example:

- Our own teeth are sentient beings that choose not to communicate with us.
- The entire world is a dream being had by a sleeping squirrel.
- Most of the universe is made up of invisible dark matter.

I accept that I am toying with you here, since the last one is currently what modern astrophysicists *do* think. It only makes sense in calculations based around gravitational fields and the like, but it is currently something that is almost impossible to disprove, because dark matter is essentially invisible. We can't detect it, but they tell us that it's there. In fact, it might even be four-fifths of the universe if you include dark matter and dark energy! Of course matter and energy are essentially the same thing in quantum physics, so that's neither here nor there. So, physicists expect us to believe that the majority of the universe is made of up an invisible thing. For the average person, that's a bit like saying it's all a big squirrel's dream. I make this point because I want to show you that sometimes even sound scientific arguments can seem like poor arguments, but that's often because we don't understand them. I'm not an astrophysicist, but I'm willing to suspend natural disbelief about the wacky things they tell us, because I know they understand it themselves (and there are tens of thousands of them). That's different from someone who tells you it's all a squirrel's dream: they are extremely unlikely to have any reasoning that makes sense to anyone except themselves.

## Shifting the burden of proof

**Shifting the burden of proof** involves turning the concept of proof on its head as a poor retort to a critic. Many of us have heard children use the same type of argument. When someone says that little Johnny could not possibly have lifted the rock up all by himself, Johnny says 'Prove it!' Of course, the burden of proof actually lies with Johnny, since he is the one claiming something unproven.

## Special pleading

**Special pleading** is a style of argument that claims a global principle, then exempts one thing from it because it is somehow special. Sometimes, it can be legitimate, but sometimes the criterion for judging the special case is irrelevant to the argument. Thus, when you try to judge a special pleading argument, always look for the relevance of the exception. For example, we fix speed limits for driving on our roads. No one is allowed to break these. However, in order for police to chase people who are driving above the speed limit, they might sometimes need to exceed the limit themselves. This is a relevant case for special pleading. However, we also have a blood-alcohol limit above which you are not allowed to drive. We don't 'special plead' this for police officers, because drinking alcohol while driving is never something a police officer might need to do in order to catch criminals.

Dictators often set rules that they don't obey themselves, because they use special pleading. However, often their special pleading is simply 'Because I am the leader'. This does not make sense in itself as a rational argument.

Another example of a poor special pleading argument is for the boss of a company to decide to cut costs by making everyone travelling on business use the cheapest tickets. However, the boss travels first class, and claims that this is a special case because he or she is the boss. Being the boss per se does not constitute a relevant criterion for special pleading. Nor would having a special parking space, for example, but bosses often do just that.

## The straw person

Originally called the 'straw man' fallacy, the **straw person** fallacy involves exaggerating or distorting the opposite opinion, thus making it easier to attack or discredit. An example might be to claim that Freud said that all problems stem from repressed sexual desires. This would be ludicrous, but it's a common misconception. In fact, Freud never said such a thing: he believed that *many* did, but many is not all.

## False binary opposition

**False binary opposition** refers to posing a choice as an either-or when this is not necessarily the case. It is often referred to as the 'false dilemma' or 'black and white dilemma'. On 20 September 2001 George W. Bush said 'Either you are with us, or you are with the terrorists'. Of course, this is not a genuine either-or: it is possible to be against terrorism *and* against Bush's campaigns in the Middle East. In fact, there are probably infinite shades of opinion in between. In psychology, be wary of people who claim that criminal behaviour is genetic *or* caused by socialisation: it's probably both. In fact, most things in psychology aren't binary.

However, we do sometimes get confused over the opposite problem. One thing in statistics is essentially truly binary, but we treat it as if it isn't: statistical significance. Let's sort this out right now. When you set an alpha level to test a hypothesis, usually 5 per cent, or .05, you *set* it. You cannot move it later, no matter what. This means that when you get a difference with a *p* value of .04, you accept the difference because its associated probability is less than the *predetermined* value of chance. If you get a *p* value of .051, what do you do? The temptation is to ramble on about a 'trend' that is 'almost' significant. However, .05 is a cut-off point: we have created a binary distinction. This means that you can't treat it like a continuous scale when it suits you later on. Either things are significant or they aren't.

Most things in the real world aren't that simple, even though we like to think that they are. Most of our binary oppositions are for convenience, but are not real. 'Hot' and 'cold', for example. When does hot become cold, or vice versa? You don't know, do you? 'Man' and 'woman' are treated like opposites, but they are just versions of a species, and some people aren't clearly one or the other, for real biological reasons, not just perceptions. 'Raw' and 'cooked' are beautiful examples. If something isn't cooked, then it's raw, isn't it? But can you decide so easily when something is cooked? Think about this kind of distinction when you research and read about psychological phenomena.

## Ad hominem fallacy

Also known as *argumentum ad hominem*, this is an example of a fallacy that finds itself being used regularly in the courtroom, for example, and is therefore something that all forensic psychologists should be aware of. It is a fallacy based on the idea that you can discredit an argument by discrediting its *source*. It's a common tactic of lawyers in rape cases, for example, to try to discredit the victim by demonstrating that they are sexually promiscuous. Now, much as this is a typical way for lawyers to proceed, it isn't valid – promiscuity isn't a justification for rape. Rape is defined as non-consensual, and promiscuity is consensual by nature. So it actually doesn't matter what the person does in their personal life – what matters is if the particular sexual act that occurred was consensual or not.

Another example of the **ad hominem** fallacy arises when we refuse to listen to a perfectly good argument because the person making it has offended us. The philosopher Nietzsche has been criticised for his politics, which it is said influenced Hitler. Does that mean that everything Nietzsche said must be dismissed because of the association with

Fascist politics and the atrocities committed by some people who read his works? Naturally, this is logically invalid, but some people do reject every word of Nietzsche's work as a result. Would you reject every word of a financial expert if you discovered that they were prosecuted for not paying their taxes? Would you fire a cleaner if you discovered that their own house was dirty, even if they did a perfectly good job on yours? Would you look down on a celebrated chef because they only ever ate burgers and pizza themselves? Sometimes it's hard to know what counts as relevant and what doesn't. However, I think I know the answer to the following question: would you take driving lessons from someone who had been prosecuted for dangerous driving? Let us make it more complicated: would you take driving lessons from someone who was prosecuted for dangerous driving twenty years ago and who since then has been a driving instructor with an impeccable record?

## Begging the question

**Begging the question**, or *petitio principii*, is the situation in which the conclusion is somehow inserted into the argument, often subtly, and is then used to substantiate the argument.

'As a mother myself, I know about child development'. You might have heard this argument before. It is a common one. Of course, this then is the start of a pronouncement based on an authority that is 'begged' from the listener rather than 'given'. Where is the evidence that being a mother means that a person knows about child development? Is certainly does not mean that they know about the generalities of child development, even if they know the specifics concerning their own child or children. Furthermore, they cannot even claim expertise in respect of their own children, since they might be mistaken about them, or indeed could have given them up for adoption years ago. They would still technically be a mother, although what they could be said to know about children might be limited. A useful trick to check the logic of such an argument is to turn it on its head, or to substitute one term for another. Would you accept the following argument: 'As a human being, I know about people'? This is tantamount to allowing someone to operate on your arthritic knee because they, too, have knees, and therefore must know about them. Being something, or possessing something, does not give you *a priori* unquestionable expertise on the subject. That must be proved elsewhere.

This also overlaps with another fallacy, which concerns questionable authority.

## *Appeal to questionable authority*

**Appeal to questionable authority**, or *argumentum ad verecundiam*, is where someone uses an authority or expertise figure to strengthen an argument. However, the expert being quoted is often not an expert at all, but someone famous, at best in a related field. On my Kellogg's® Frosties packet I see a picture of footballer Ian Wright. Next to his smiling face, I read the following: 'FACT: Children who eat cereal for breakfast each day are less likely to be overweight than those who don't'. There is, admittedly, a small-print asterisk, and on the reverse of the packet a reference to the source, 'de la Hunty (2006)', writing in the *Nutrition Bulletin*. I personally cannot find a single-author article by 'de la Hunty' in that journal in that year, and the one I can find is by three authors and is not relevant. There *is* an article in 2007 in the *Nutrition Bulletin*, by De La Hunty, so perhaps it is nothing more than an understandable misprint. Furthermore, it isn't a single authored piece, but is actually De La Hunty and Ashwell (2007). It's a systematic review of the evidence to show that people who eat breakfast cereals are slimmer than those who do not. The authors found 'consistent evidence' of a relationship between eating breakfast cereal and having a healthy weight, but said that there was 'limited evidence' for a mechanism that would lead to the conclusion that this relationship was causal. To quote from the abstract: 'The relationship could arise out of confounding by lifestyle factors'. In other words, it is possible that people who eat cereal for breakfast happen to be the same kind of people who exercise regularly, eat fruit and vegetables and avoid calorie-laden, refined and processed foodstuffs. The research was sponsored by Kellogg's; I found that on the company's website.

Arguably, therefore, Ian Wright is serving only as a front man. Of course, this might cause some people to ask why we need a famous footballer to tell us what nutrition experts said about eating cereal for breakfast. Exercising critical thinking, one might also apply Socratic questioning, and ask 'What exactly is a *fact*? Are we satisfied with the definition of "fact" as used in this context?' Yes, children who eat breakfast are less likely to be overweight than those who don't. However, if you suddenly take overweight children and force them to eat breakfast, it won't necessarily mean that they lose weight: they may well get fatter.

In essence, that is what the authors of the systematic review seem to be saying when they say that lifestyle issues confound the relationship between eating cereals for breakfast and maintaining a healthy weight.

This leads us to consider Socratic questioning in a little more detail.

# SOCRATIC QUESTIONING: THE ANCIENT ART OF 'BUT WHY?'

For some, Socratic questioning is at the heart of critical thinking. Socrates encouraged probing arguments by tearing them apart with a series of questions. It's the philosophical equivalent of a child who constantly asks 'But why?' to everything you say. They take a number of forms, but those below are the main ones.

**Questions of clarification**   What are you getting at? What do you mean by 'insight'? What exactly is the way forward?

**Questions to probe assumptions**   Why are you assuming that X causes Y? Am I right that you are assuming that this is the case? What would happen if we assume the opposite for a moment?

**Questions about points of view**   Do you agree or disagree with that? What is your belief? Why did you make that inference?

**Questions about evidence**   Why is that happening? How do we know that is the case? Can you show me how that works?

**Questions about implications and consequences**   What would happen if that is taken to its logical conclusion? Will this cause that? What are you implying by that statement?

**Questions about the question**   Why ask that question? Is this the right thing to ask? Is there something else we ought to look for?

A combination of these questions can be the basis for a critique, or indeed a discussion in class. What is important is that we are asking questions, not only of the authors of an argument, but of ourselves in

addressing and attacking that argument. Socratic questions tell us as much about ourselves as they do about the subject at hand: they are at the heart of reflective practice.

## WHY PRIORITISE CRITICAL THINKING?

Students could legitimately ask why critical thinking is so important. After all, lecturers like me want them to challenge assumptions, applying Socratic questioning to the very reasons for including critical thinking in our marking criteria.

One reason that is particularly important for psychology is that critical thinking overlaps with the scientific method, something we lecturers clearly want our students to understand and employ. It is about the production of evidence to verify assumptions, and it is about applying logic, both numerate and literate, to solve problems. In fact, critical thinking also overlaps with problem solving. Again, problem solving is something we expect our students to handle well.

Browne and Keeley (2007) refer to 'the sponge' and 'panning for gold' as distinct approaches to thinking and to study. The sponge soaks up everything until it is full: panning for gold involves the patient and methodical sifting through everything until the nuggets of value emerge. The latter, by analogy, is critical thinking. One might argue that some traditional examination systems encourage sponging and give too little credit for panning for gold. When you demand critical thinking of students, you redress that balance somewhat.

I would not want you to think, however, that the scientific method is something that all psychologists believe in without question. There is a body of psychologists set up to question everything. They go by various names, including 'postmodernists', 'social constructionists' and 'critical psychologists'. I'm not claiming that all of these amount to the same thing, because there are differences, but it's also the case that they tend to share a view that calls science into question, and attacks the notion of progress and development. It doesn't do us any harm to question ourselves, and science has suffered from a lot of pomposity over the centuries. Psychology isn't perfect; not all of it is or can be 'scientific', and we ought to realise that. However, it's a two-way street. The criticisms that we can apply to science we can also apply to anti-science. If there's no such thing as truth and progress, then that applies equally to the criticisms of science! You can't have your cake and eat it, as they say. Think back to the fallacy surrounding special pleading. It isn't valid to say that science is flawed because science is a human construction, like almost everything apart from flowers and rocks, and then say that the claims you make are exempt from this. If everything is a social construction, and ultimately flawed, then *everything* is – including the statement that everything is a social construction.

## CHAPTER 2 – CRITICAL QUESTIONS

1. How can a knowledge of Socratic questioning help you to write essays?
2. Choose an argument from a source such as a blog, and apply your understanding of logical fallacies to it. How well does it stand up?

# 3  Critical Thinking in the Wider World

## AM I BOVVERED?

Examples of poor logic abound in popular culture, and unfortunately many children and quite a few adults resort to shoddy arguments, or even fail to argue completely. This shows a lack of critical thinking.

When Catherine Tate's famous schoolgirl character (Lauren Cooper, *The Catherine Tate Show*, BBC) resorts to saying 'Am I bovvered?' in response to criticisms, she displays a perfect example of an argument without substance (as did Tony Blair in the *Comic Relief* special, turning the character's comments back at her). Whether a diversionary tactic or a failing of logic, her stock answer is actually no answer at all to the charge levelled at her, whatever it is. If her essay is late, she asks if she looks bothered. If she can't work out how long it takes ten men to dig a hole six feet by three feet by four feet, she says she isn't bothered. Of course, how bothered she is or isn't is in no way a relevant factor. Or is it?

On the surface, she is flaunting Grice's Maxim of Relevance. The philosopher of language Paul Grice (1989) identified conversational maxims (truths or rules) that normally must be adhered to for discourse to work. However, this is not always the case. The classic example is when someone asks someone out on a date and their answer is 'I'm washing my hair'. On the surface, this is entirely irrelevant. It is not an answer to 'Would you like to have dinner with me later this week?' However, we all know that it *is* an answer. So, when Catherine Tate's character says 'Am I bovvered?' she effectively is saying something else. She is, of course, stating that the entire premise of the questioner's or accusator's comments is ill-founded, and that their preoccupation with the issue at hand is somehow petty or unnecessary. The essay might be late, but in the scheme of things a late essay is of no consequence, which is why she 'Ain't bovvered'.

Vicky Pollard, Matt Lucas' rambling West Country schoolgirl character in BBC's *Little Britain*, a character preceding that of Tate but remarkably comparable in some ways, does a similar thing. However, she doesn't so much belittle the argument she is faced with as attempt to befuddle with **rhetoric**. If she is told her essay is late, her first answer is always 'Yeah, but, no, but, yeah'. On the face of it, it is another example of a complete lack of reasoning ability. Equally, however, it could represent a questioning of the premise that the essay is actually late. Perhaps she is explaining that the essay is late in one sense, but not late in another? Furthermore, when pressed, she often says something like 'There's this whole other thing what you don't know nuffink about so just shut up'. What she is doing is claiming extenuating circumstances. Of course, the reasons for her late essay are usually flouting the Maxim of Relevance too. Typically, her excuses revolve around some entirely unconnected series of seemingly non-linear events involving her friends and their antics.

The humour invoked by these characters probably arises because they remind us of the flawed logic so commonly used by children. This includes the wonderful example of a rhetorical circularity, as in the case in which a child, asked to explain why they love the *Harry Potter* books, answers 'Because they are really good'. This is common (try it on any seven-year old), but entirely devoid of an answer. By definition, something one likes is really good. The 'answer' is, therefore, simply restating the proposition. I estimate that around 90 per cent of TV interviews with children are like this. It makes one wonder why interviewers bother asking children their opinions. Cute they might be, entertaining, yes, but informative rarely. Sometimes, children do, of course, make very intelligent and useful contributions. When they don't, apply your critical thinking skills to the act of the editor including their comments in the piece. Why have they been included? Are they filling time, or putting them there for entertainment? It's no different to those occasions when an adult says something downright stupid that is not edited out. One is drawn to the conclusion that the comments have been included for entertainment value.

Adults can fall foul of saying silly things all the time without even realising it, in the form of subtle **hyperbole**. In linguistic terms, *hyperbole* is the repetition of an idea within a phrase. Most of us have never stopped to wonder why we say 'free gift', when a gift is free by definition.

Similarly, it's not possible to have anything but a 'mass exodus', since an 'exodus' is a mass movement: 'exodus' alone will do. Similarly, 'pizza pie' is meaningless to an Italian, since it simply means 'pie pie'. As another example, a 'gambit' is an opening move, so 'opening gambit' is a rather ridiculous thing to say. Equally, you cannot have a 'main protagonist', since a protagonist is a main character. Next time you kneel down, think about it. You can't kneel up, so the 'down' is not needed at all. One last example: 'It will happen in two minutes, time'. The word 'time' is unnecessary. And we haven't even got to the problem of people saying '110 per cent' yet.

If you're wondering where all this is going, it's quite simple. Critical thinking is what got me here. As the writer, I sat down, thought about things, shook them up, turned them on their heads and presented them to you in a slightly different light. This section is an example of critical thinking. I examined the commonplace, the everyday, and said something new about it. Of course, if you didn't agree with anything I said in this section, you're probably engaging with me in a bout of reciprocal critical thinking. That's not a bad thing.

# MORE ABOUT GRICE'S MAXIMS

We've mentioned one of Grice's Maxims, but in fact there are four. These are Quality, Quantity, Relevance and Manner. In fact, whenever you make an argument or judge someone else's, think about that argument in the light of these maxims. Relevance we have already dealt with: you should stick to the subject and not veer off. The Maxim of Quantity states that you should say just enough to make your point, no more or less, and include enough information to support your argument, but not overload the reader. The Maxim of Quality states that you should only make statements that you believe to be true and avoid statements lacking evidence.

Finally, we have the Maxim of Manner. This states that you should be as clear as possible. If your argument falls down, it should be because there's a better way of looking at things, not because it's too complicated or confusing for anyone else to understand. There are a lot of websites you might like to look at that will give you examples of arguments that most of us seem to struggle to understand, and you can find them easily if you search for them. I have some of my own favourites, but I won't suggest them to you because I want you to experience the joys and horrors of just how bizarre some people's ideas are. One place to start, however, is the Rational Wiki website, which features criticisms, more or less humorous, of all sorts of strange and complicated arguments. Its section on 'cranks' is worth a look.

# THE ARTS

In the light of our growing understanding of the nature of critical thinking, it is now time to consider another common phenomenon. You will probably have your own opinions on the subject, but have you actually subjected your opinion to any analysis or criticism? The answer is probably 'no'.

Saying 'the arts' rather than just 'art' means that I can use examples from music and dance, for instance, not just painting or sculpture. Over and over again we read and hear about the same old issue in the arts. Someone produces a work of modern art and it polarises opinion. Some people find value in it; others dismiss it. The same thing applies across all media, even though it is sculpture and painting that often attracts the most publicity.

Tracey Emin's *My Bed* is an example of a work that generated some negative reactions. It consists of a rather dirty, stained bed. That's pretty much it, on the surface. Much earlier, Marcel Duchamp's work *Fountain*, the most famous of his 'readymades', is simply a urinal placed in a gallery and signed.

One of the most interesting conceptual artists falling into the genre of the controversial is Martin Creed. His works include:

- Work No. 227, the lights going on and off.
- Work No. 88, a sheet of A4 paper crumpled into a ball.
- Work No. 990, a curtain opening and closing.

In case you are wondering, the descriptions really do sum up the actual work itself. Some would say that Creed's pieces stretch the definition of art as far as it is possible to go. Some of his works might seem ridiculous, but there is something quite striking about them, and they certainly generate a reaction. Those who oppose such work commonly express their distaste for it by proclaiming that it 'isn't art'. Let us examine this claim.

The view that a pile of rubble, or a toilet, or a bed, or some paper, placed in a gallery, is 'not art' is often based upon a reaction, often instant. Because it is instantaneous, the reaction is usually emotional rather than cognitive. Cognitive reactions take longer to form than emotional ones. We see a painting or sculpture and we 'feel' something about it. Over time, maybe minutes, but often hours or even years, we see it differently.

Everyone, of course, is entitled to whatever reaction they have, and they are not obliged to spend a single second of their lives musing over a particular piece of art: this is a given. However, the moment someone makes a proclamation about a work, they have engaged with it. Once they have engaged, their opinion is, naturally, subject to scrutiny and challenge. If you have no opinion on something, I cannot disagree with you. The moment you voice an opinion, I can choose to agree or disagree, or to investigate your opinion. You've thrown your hat into the ring, as it were. Some people use an interesting trick when the going gets tough. They offer an opinion, then when their opinion is criticised, they say 'I was only giving my opinion', as if that meant that their comments are not to be criticised. Think about this for a moment. If you are 'only' giving your opinion, then what is it for? This is tantamount to saying 'I am just saying some words which are not intended to be a contribution to the conversation in any way'. Of course, when was the last time you heard someone say 'I was only voicing my opinion' after someone agreed with them? It is only ever used as a weak defence to a criticism.

Let us get back, then, to the opinion that something 'isn't art'. When you interrogate people on such a claim, their justifications tend to consist of one or more of the following:

- It is not art because it is distasteful or offensive.
- It is not art because it is not pleasing or satisfying.
- It is not art because it looks as if it was easy to create.
- It is not art because it isn't like other art that I recognise.
- It is not art because I don't understand it.

Let us examine each of these viewpoints critically.

## Offence in art

The view that a work can be excluded from the category of 'art' because it causes offence works only on an entirely personal level, at a fixed point in time. What do I mean by this? Well, what offends me can change over time, so if I object to something because I am offended, then in 20 years I might feel differently anyway. Similarly, there are things that might have offended me 20 years ago which don't any more. This is very odd, because I am effectively proclaiming that a particular painting is not art now, but it might be later on. That sounds like a very strange position to take.

It is true that we change our minds over time, however. Very few people today find the works of the Impressionists either offensive or unworthy of the label 'art'. In fact, we have come so far that we now view these works as the very embodiment of art. At the time, however, they were offensive to a great many people, who saw the styles of painting as an abomination. People said that Monet wasn't producing art, or Renoir, Sisley or Pissarro. That they caused *offence* by their works is not too strong a way of putting it, but today's rebellion is often tomorrow's mainstream. Adut (2008) gives over a whole section of a book to the scandals associated with the Impressionist movement. So, by saying that something offends you now, you really aren't able to make the claim that this prevents it from being art.

Of course, I might feel that I never change, and so offence is offence, and I will always be offended by something. If I dismiss art based upon this, it must be entirely personal, since I cannot claim to speak for everyone else on the highly subjective nature of offence. What offends me isn't what offends everyone. I would even go as far as to say that this cannot possibly be the grounds for dismissing works of art, because there is probably not a single piece of art in existence that someone, somewhere, wouldn't find offensive. The world is very diverse, and no matter how odd an opinion, somebody probably holds it somewhere.

The next argument is to say that if something offends 'enough' people it isn't art. Now we are getting somewhere, perhaps. However, if you try to define the word 'enough', you can't. You would probably end up going for 'majority', but that doesn't mean that the majority is right. Furthermore, how major must the majority be? Would 501 people in 1000 be 'enough'? Is that really fair on the 499 people who aren't offended and want to see the work on public display?

There is a second issue that is arguably more important. Some people claim that offending people is a distinct *purpose* of art. By offending, the artist generates a reaction, makes people discuss and debate issues, and so this is one of the definitions of what art is! This argument leads us to believe that offending people is a good thing. Look at the face of a person who is shocked or offended. Are their eyes not open wider than usual? Do they not see more as a result?

## Aesthetics in art

This argument boils down to saying that something is not art because you don't like it. Using critical thinking tools, I can dismiss this quickly. I like the tool of substitution: take the same sentence structure and replace certain key words. Then you'll see exactly why this doesn't work:

- Jazz isn't music, because I don't like it.
- Broccoli isn't food, because I don't like it.
- Yellow isn't a colour, because I don't like it.

As you see, this simply isn't an argument. If I don't like something, it is only an issue for me; other people might like it. As long as they do, and they agree that the particular painting is art, then I can't claim that it isn't on the grounds of personal taste or preference.

## Talent in art

The film *My Kid Could Paint That* documents the controversial paintings done by a small child from the USA that sold for many thousands of dollars. It caused all manner of speculation about the artist, including doubts as to whether her father was somehow 'directing' the art to the extent that the talent lay with him, not with the child herself. We have also seen examples of animals such as apes or elephants creating art. You can even write computer programs that create art. The National Gallery of Art in Washington, DC has an online painting program, BRUSHster. You can load it, press the 'auto' button and watch it create a piece of abstract art that you can then meddle with digitally. The amount of talent required is minimal.

To many, an artist needs to display talent to be taken seriously; for others, the end product is all that matters. If the end product inspires a reaction, does it matter how much hard work or talent went into it? There is simply no answer this question: it is a matter of opinion. This is one of the most important lessons to learn in critical thinking. You need to develop the skill to discriminate between something you can dissect, examine and debate, and something that is simply a matter of opinion and which no amount of discussion or examination will alter. When something is a matter of opinion, arguably you are better finding something else on which to use your critical thinking skills.

You could argue that most things are a matter of opinion; that's probably true. Does this mean that there's no point in applying critical thinking? No, because most things involve a mixture of facts, statements about things and opinions. Furthermore, opinions vary in the extent to which we can criticise them. Some opinions are entirely open to critical thinking, but some aren't. In the example above I am discussing those opinions that can't be examined further. When you reach that point, there really is no way to move. If someone says that talent is important in determining art, the only place to go is to state the opposite opinion, or to move the argument to one side and discuss the nature of talent. In fact, that's what I recommend in this case. If someone says that art is about talent, ask them to define 'talent'. There's a rich seam to mine there.

## Comparative art

It is perfectly understandable that as thinking beings we judge things by comparing them to familiar exemplars; if we didn't, we would never recognise anything in front of us. However, if we use this comparative judgement as the basis for defining art, we instantly hit a problem. Comparisons effectively stifle creativity, which for art is a considerable problem, given that art is a creative endeavour. What I mean by this is that if we define art as something *recognisable* as art, then genuinely innovative and creative ideas are jettisoned in favour of the familiar and well-established. In short, if you dismiss art you don't recognise, art does not progress, which few would agree makes much sense. Therefore, the argument that something isn't art because it doesn't share the values or characteristics of previous art only works if art is meant to be static. If art is supposed to change with the times, and be a truly creative endeavour, then new work is to be lauded and appreciated, not rejected because it isn't as good as something else, or doesn't follow a particular tradition or trend.

## Understanding art

One can easily sympathise with the view that something incomprehensible lacks value. It is, perhaps, a natural reaction to imponderable things to cast them aside and ignore them. It is often the case that people view 'modern art' as something about which they just say 'I don't get it'. It is a short step, perhaps, from 'I don't get it' to 'It isn't art' – except, of course, that this is an example of a *non sequitur* argument. It is quite illogical to claim that a work is not art because you personally do not understand it. Someone else might, and even if no one does, art is not something one necessarily needs to understand. Art is not like mathematics homework.

Furthermore, the assumption here is that the person who dismisses art that they do not understand actually understands the art they do like. Even the most obvious representational painting (that of a bowl of fruit, for example) often has so much more meaning within it than the obvious. Yes, it is a painting of a bowl of fruit, but is that *all* that it is? Why those fruit, in that configuration, painted in that way, and so on? There is much to ponder, and a great deal to fail to understand in even the most 'simple' of artworks.

## Final comments on art

People who claim that something is not art are in trouble from the outset, because that statement cannot be accepted without following it up. If you claim that something is not art, you must surely know what art is. After all, I *know* that a lemon is not a kangaroo. How?

Because I know what a kangaroo is. It has a certain weight, size, shape, a pouch, a certain colour and so on. A lemon has virtually nothing in common with a kangaroo, except that it is a biological, organic object. But if I say that something is not art, I must therefore define art: the onus (or burden of proof) is on me to do so. I have yet to meet anyone who can do this satisfactorily without contradicting themselves somewhere if pressed on the issue. When someone defines art, they often do so using the characteristics described above, which we have just shown to be difficult to substantiate.

Once more I must make it clear that everyone is entitled to an opinion. However, everyone is also entitled to challenge opinions, to make judgements on the basis of those opinions, and to attach value to those opinions that allow further thought and opinion to develop.

It is my own view, therefore, that some opinions about art make more sense than others. Perhaps you are entitled to your opinion, no matter how much sense it makes? Maybe so. However, you are reading a book on critical thinking, which means that you really are interested in finding ways to examine ideas and to attach value to those ideas. Fundamentally, critical thinking is about taking things apart, seeing what makes them tick, then judging them in some way based upon what they contain. Some ideas, statements, thoughts and opinions *are* more useful, valuable or sensible than others. I would contest that in the case of art those people who dismiss something by claiming that it is not art are on considerably shakier ground than those who are happy to accept *anything* as art.

There is a way to rescue the opinion that something isn't art from the scrapheap of unjustified nonsense. Quite simply, add 'to me' to the end of the statement. 'This isn't art *to me*' is a completely different comment from 'This isn't art'. I suspect that this is what most people really mean, but if we are thinking critically we really must be careful about what we express. What we *mean* is not something others get access to, except through what we *say*. Therefore, we must try to say what we mean.

# APPLYING CRITICAL THINKING TO THE LANGUAGE OF ADVERTISING

A cynical person might say that a great deal of advertising is about selling you something you don't need, or selling you something you do need at the highest possible price. In many countries there are rules and laws which prevent advertisers from lying to the public. However, the wily advertiser will always look to find ways around these. It would be illegal to claim that a skin product *will* make you look 20 years younger. But it is perfectly acceptable to rephrase this by asserting that the same product *could help* you to look 20 years younger. The difference comes in the use of the word 'could', which is much less definite than the word 'will'. In addition, 'could help' is even more wishy-washy, if you like, so that the watering down of the claims becomes perfectly legal, even though the average person might not actually notice, when reading quickly, the difference between the two types of statement.

Advertisers are very aware of the kinds of words that they can and cannot use, and the different situations and scenarios that allow them to stay within the law but subtly make all sorts of claims about products. As a critical thinker, you should start to look carefully at the language used in various advertising media, such as TV, radio, newspapers and so on. You will soon start to notice just how common the subtle plays on words actually are. 'Might' is one of the words that are used time and time again to say absolutely nothing but to suggest a great deal. Reading this book *might* make you rich. Reading this book *might* make you feel sick. Reading this book *might* make you jump in the air, pretend to be a dog, and develop a rash all over your arms that can only be cured by applying tomato soup to the affected areas. As you can see, just about anything *might* happen, which makes saying it rather pointless. Some things are extremely improbable, but they *might* happen. Add the word 'help' to this and, if it were possible, you have instantly made the pointless word 'might' even more pointless.

Another common word that is used to mean nothing is 'fight'. Medically, for instance, 'fight' means virtually nothing. I can fight and fight and fight but it does not mean that I will win. 'Cure' is another story altogether. If I have a product that I claim can cure asthma, then I must have evidence to show that it does. However, if I say I have a product that *helps to fight* asthma, the burden of proof is now tiny. If I now say I have a product which *might help to fight* asthma, then in legal terms I'm saying almost nothing at all – but would the average consumer realise this?

Pick up a magazine and flick through the advertisements. Identify the language used, then reflect on just how little is being truly communicated. Identify also the miscommunications that advertisements often rely on. Furthermore, where 'evidence' for claims is cited, look carefully at that evidence, using your psychologist's research methods skills. It's not unusual to find that the evidence consists of a study in which 39 women were asked if their skin was 'better' after using a particular moisturiser, and 27 of them said 'yes'. How many things can you find that are wrong with this?

The words that we use to stretch the truth, as it were, are often referred to as *weasel words*. They allow us to make claims, then weasel out of criticism by saying that we meant something different from the way in which people interpreted what we said. They are, essentially, legal loopholes in themselves. How often have you noticed a sale that was advertised as 'up to 75 per cent off'? Off what? And 'up to' means that only one product has to be reduced by three quarters – the rest can be kept at the same prices as before the sale! Backing off from a claim and saying 'That's not what I said/meant' is known as *tergiversation*.

# AMBIGUITY

You should always look carefully at arguments containing ambiguity of various types. Linguists and philosophers make all sorts of distinctions between types of ambiguity, but you needn't worry about these unless you are particularly fascinated. What you should be aware of is how ambiguity can be used to say one thing and claim that another is meant. Innuendo and *double entendre* are examples of this. If you want to say something rude or morally dubious, or even just flirtatious, you can hide this in seemingly innocent language. We've all probably done this accidentally in the past, and many of us have done it on purpose. A lot of humour, especially that which is found in the old British *Carry On* series of films, relies heavily on it. However, ambiguity is also used in all sorts of serious ways, sometimes to protect the speaker from later accusations.

Imagine a politician saying 'I am against quick decisions which hurt people'. What exactly does this mean? Are they saying that quick decisions hurt people, and therefore they are against making them? Or are they saying that they are perfectly comfortable with quick decisions, but they are against the ones that hurt people? It's quite a big distinction.

In psychology, ambiguity pervades everything, and in research we must do everything that we can to avoid it. For example, gestures are often ambiguous, without even mentioning the fact that they differ from culture to culture or nation to nation. For example, the 'OK' gesture, with thumb and finger curled to make an 'o', is used all over the world, but *never* use this in Brazil: it's extremely offensive. Whenever we conduct observational studies, the very subject matter of our observations is potentially ambiguous from start to finish. Technically, so are transcripts of interviews that we analyse in qualitative studies. We don't know what people really *mean* to convey; the text is everything, and all that we have, but we all lack clarity sometimes. Some scientists might deliberately try to obfuscate things by 'hiding' inconvenient findings in ambiguous statements or graphical representations. Always ask yourself what the purpose of simplicity and clarity really is. Primarily, it's about avoiding ambiguity.

# LIBEL AND THE LAW

Just as advertisers are careful about what they say, skirting around the line between acceptable and unacceptable descriptions of products and services, so must journalists writing for newspapers or presenting the news on TV be careful to try to present a story without being sued. There are various ways to do this, and the law around libel and slander (including defamation of character) is extremely sensitive and fraught. Although there are no cast-iron, guaranteed ways to avoid being taken to Court for saying something about someone, some words are safer than others. Look out for 'It has been suggested that . . .', 'We understand that . . .' and 'Rumours abound that . . .' This kind of language is worth being aware of, because although it is often used to avoid legal problems when essentially saying something fairly awful, you can use it yourself to soften arguments and avoid using the first person too heavily in your work. There is a world of difference in tone and force between 'I think that Baddeley is wrong' and 'Some people might say that Baddeley is wrong'.

Keep your ears open for other ways to soften your language. One of my favourites is 'What do you say to those people who say X, Y and Z about you?' You'll hear that quite a lot from journalists talking to politicians and celebrities. What it means, in essence, is 'You are X, Y and Z. What do you make of that?' Given that X, Y and Z is often something like 'a liar, a cheat and a moron', you can see why it helps to alter the language around it!

# WHEN IS A REVIEW NOT A REVIEW?

We are all familiar these days with online reviews of products. Websites such as those of Amazon or software such as iTunes®, for example, commonly feature public reviews of products, including books and music. However, if you look closely at these, many of them are actually not reviews at all, but opinions. Some of them are not even disguised.

A review should tell you something about a product that you didn't know before, and give you a better understanding. Therefore, the first non-review I will draw your attention to is the unqualified opinion, then we will turn to some of the more sophisticated non-reviews.

## *The unqualified opinion*

When we use the phrase 'unqualified opinion', this does not mean that the *reviewer* is unqualified. This is important for you to understand, and is often a source of confusion. It is the *opinion* that is unqualified, because in this context 'unqualified' means 'without explanation'.

Children commonly give unqualified reviews when asked about things they like or dislike, and the least useful unqualified opinion is to restate the obvious. For example:

Q: *'Why do you like this book?'*
A: *'Because it is good.'*

This means absolutely nothing. It is of no use at all as a review, nor is the answer even an answer! It's common for children to do this because they are still developing their critical skills, but most people 'grow out of' this kind of answer. However, you'll find these unqualified opinions all over the internet disguised as reviews.

*'This is the best album ever.'*
*'This music blows me away.'*
*'Simply the worst book I have ever read.'*

The first two of these are impossible to put into any context. Firstly, it is quite illegitimate to claim that something is the 'best ever' unless you are familiar with everything that came before it. This reviewer, literally, is claiming to have heard all albums ever produced in history. We should therefore ignore this, since it is bound to be founded on a lie.

The second example only helps me if I know what kind of thing 'blows away' this person. Knowing what their emotional reaction is does provide me with a little information, but nothing I can use. For all I know, this person gets 'blown away' by the dull sound of a peeled carrot dropping into a bowl of flour.

The last of these 'reviews' is particularly interesting. There are two things we must know in order to make use of this review. The first is the basis for saying the book concerned is 'the worst'. Worst written? Worst printed? The worst story, worst character development, worst value for money? There are hundreds of possibilities. But, more worryingly, we have no idea how many books this person has read. If they have read thousands, then I might start to listen. However, for all I know, they have only ever read two books. The 'worst' of two is hardly worth knowing.

Sites such as YouTube® also feature video comments, and these are also interesting to look at from a critical thinking perspective. Some of these correspond to nothing more than an insult, such as a single word (often 'lame'), or two words ('this sucks'). More favourable comments are often nothing more than 'this is cool' or 'awesome'. As comments, they actually add nothing to the video they attempt to describe.

## The unfair review

It is remarkably common to see reviews that unfairly slam a product because the reviewer received a faulty one. For example, 'I bought this for my son. When it arrived, it would not even switch on and I had to send it back. Avoid this.'

One is naturally frustrated by a product that doesn't work. Most of us have experienced this, and it can be angering and time-consuming. However, a small proportion of units of anything that is manufactured do not work. Saying this is not actually a review of the product *per se*. Are we to assume that, because the particular unit this person received was faulty, all units are faulty? This is a serious flaw in thinking. Very few legitimate companies create a product without testing it and send out thousands and thousands of units onto the market that do not work. We know this, partly because any company that did so would be bankrupt in a matter of weeks. We accept that now and then products do not work, and actually the customer service process behind the return of a faulty item is much more useful to know about. If the company takes years to answer your letters or e-mails, or never refunds a customer's money, you need to know. This would be information worth adding to a review. However, to suggest that someone should not buy a particular radio because you bought one that didn't work is ludicrous.

Why not explore various sites, hunting down these types of reviews? You won't be searching long before you find one. When you do, why not tick the little box that says that the review wasn't helpful, if there is one? This is your way of balancing the review with your opinion of the review and its quality.

## The wrong end of the stick

I have often found comments or reviews in which the person providing the text has simply misunderstood the purpose of the thing they are reviewing. This is common when an online video is a parody or spoof of something else. One often sees comments that imply that the video is a 'rip-off' of the original, where the person has kindly pointed out the source. Similarly, I have encountered comments that imply that the reviewer has taken something completely seriously that is intended as a joke. There is a famous spoof US newspaper called *The Onion* that has now branched out into spoof news broadcasts. These are very well produced, and often quite subtly ridiculous: it's hard to explain unless you've seen what they do. You will find them if you search on sites like YouTube.

However, the fact that these video clips are so good at parody means that some people watch them and think that they are real. One example concerns a hoax that claims that the US has given billions of dollars of aid to the rich nation of Andorra because they thought it was in Africa. The government spokesman blamed the Andorran people for this, because 'They knew where they were'. I have seen a number of comments on this video that clearly indicate that people have been outraged and upset by this 'news'. It is the minority, thankfully, but some people do get sucked in.

## Irrelevance and axe grinding

Sometimes reviews veer massively off the subject and are either irrelevant or become a platform for the particular issue they want to write about. For example, many internet video reviews rapidly degenerate into racist, sexist or homophobic arguments about the people featured in the video, or more widely about entire sections of society. This can happen very quickly. For example, in the case of a comedy video that happens to feature a black person, a review comments that the video is unfunny and poor, then immediately claims that this is because the person is black. Straight away, the thread of argument completely moves away from the piece concerned and becomes political and, frankly, irrelevant in the context. Be aware of this when it happens; it can often be subtler. Have you ever read a longer article, for example, or perhaps a whole book, that starts off being about one thing and ends up being about something else entirely? In a novel this is fine, and is really just poetic licence. In terms of critical thinking applied to a piece of non-fiction, however, this shifting of emphasis and purpose is not legitimate, because it involves directing the focus away from the original point, and one should always wonder what is behind this. It's either lazy, or the author is trying to distract you.

Drifting away from the original point is often referred to as 'mission drift' or 'mission creep'; in the case of research or other projects, it is often called 'scope creep'. When you write an essay you should be aware of creep, because it is a sure-fire way to lose marks. When you are set a question, answer the question. Anything else is mission drift.

One interesting take on mission drift comes from Mike Godwin, an American internet lawyer, who pointed out that the longer a discussion or debate goes on, the probability that someone will mention the Nazis or Hitler approaches unity. That is, all debates will eventually involve someone saying something like 'You're a Nazi' or 'That's like what the Nazis did' at some point. Interestingly enough, rumour being what it is, this has been changed over time, so that some people now think that he initially said that the moment the Nazis or Hitler are mentioned, debate is effectively dead. That wasn't his original comment at all, and in a short time a form of drift occurred in relation to his original comment describing drift. That is ironic in itself.

# OCCAM'S RAZOR

Fourteenth-century English logician and friar William of Ockham first posited this important tool in the critical thinking armoury. Occam (or Ockham) put forward a rule of thumb stating that, when you have to develop a theory, you should develop the simplest possible one that matches the facts. This is why we refer to it as **Occam's Razor**: one should literally shave away everything that is unnecessary. In modern usage, we would say that, *all other things being equal,* the simplest answer is preferable to more complicated ones. Obviously, you should not select a simple answer if it doesn't make sense or fails to explain the facts. However, if you have two answers, both of which offer good explanations, choose the least complicated of the two.

Occam's Razor doesn't always work, because sometimes the most complicated explanation is actually the most appropriate one, but more often than not it does work. Note that the issue of explaining the facts is a crucial one. Supernatural explanations can be remarkably simple, for example, but they often don't explain the facts directly. One can explain almost anything by saying it is 'magical', but this takes us no further. This is the simplest explanation, but it is a very limited account of the facts. Similarly, many scientists will say that explaining things by saying that 'God did it' is equivalent to saying that 'Something did it'. Whether true or not, it doesn't allow us to make predictions or examine things further. This is why Occam's Razor must be always applied to explanations of the facts, not to *substitutes* for explanations of the facts. Keep your theories simple, and only expand on them when the facts demand it.

We can now turn to a contentious issue where Occam's Razor comes in handy.

# THE GREAT EXAMINATION DEBATE

If you want something to exercise your critical thinking muscles, you need look no further than the ongoing annual controversy in the UK concerning grade inflation and 'dumbing down' of our GCSE and A-Level assessment systems. For the benefit of those from outside of the UK, the GCSE examinations are normally taken at age 16, and the A-Levels two years later prior to going to university. They constitute the public examinations system in the UK, and are the subject of argument every year, because for a couple of decades it has appeared that more and more people have been achieving higher and higher grades. In fact, there is some evidence that grade inflation is a worldwide problem. In the UK at the time of writing, however, it seems that average grades have risen for 28 years in a row. If this carries on it will be only a matter of a few years before everyone achieves the highest possible grades. The 'solution' appears to be to invent higher grades, such as the A-star. To quote someone writing on one of the many internet forums on this subject, 'Would you trust a coin that landed heads up 27 times in succession?' There must be a reason for this astonishing, systematic increase in student success. Whatever your opinions on this subject, the arguments raised are fascinating from the perspective of logic and critical thinking. It is for this reason I discuss them here.

The classic argument against those who complain about grade inflation is stunningly irrelevant. This is the resort to 'hard work' as an explanation for the results. The claim is that the increased grades, year on year, are a result of hard work. Of course, this assumes that people sitting examinations today are working harder than those 28 years ago. Not only that, but it also assumes that this applies year on year since the 1980s. Every single year, we are being told that people are working harder. This is a strange argument, but difficult to actually disprove, since no one measures how hard people work for their examinations. However, that alone is not a reason to accept the assertion. We have absolutely no reason to assume that young people today work any *less* hard than their parents or grandparents, but we equally have no reason to assume that they work *harder*. In fact, the safest assumption is that, as human beings with examinations in front of us, we have always worked the same amount. Using Occam's Razor, hard work is not the best explanation of the facts, as we will see.

The next fallacious argument is that the quality of teaching explains the year-on-year rise in results. Of course, one would hope that teachers are as good as they have always been, if not better. One would also hope that over time teaching would improve as our understanding of education and learning improves. However, would this explain the year-on-year increases for 28 years? Probably not.

Jealousy is also not a good argument against the critics, but it does crop up regularly in commentaries on the subject. It is not unusual to hear those defending grade inflation claim that the critics are simply jealous of the achievements of today's students, or that they are simply old-fashioned in their attitudes. Of course, this is to assume the intentions and motivations of one's critics, which is hardly fair. If you criticise me, my answer cannot be to resort to assuming you have an underhand reason for doing so: it is simply not a legitimate retort unless I can produce the evidence to support it. Who knows what emotional 'baggage' is attached to the argument on both sides of this issue? Does it explain the facts? It does not, and so Occam's Razor would cause us to ignore this answer.

So, perhaps the answer to grade inflation is that students work harder *and* they are more intelligent *and* teachers are better. Potentially, all of these things are happening, and the combination of these explains the phenomenon. Now we are approaching something more credible. Most things in life are *multivariate* – that is, lots of variables together account for things that happen. Adding all three things together is a good example of thinking critically. However, thinking critically in return, one has to question the basis of all three factors. Do we have evidence that these things are actually true? Only if that is the case can we argue that in combination they explain the observations we have made. We have already said that we have no evidence that people study harder these days. We also have no evidence that people are more intelligent, except for the grades. We can't use those, because that would be an example of arguing something from its own premise: we cannot argue that people are more intelligent because their grades are higher, which explains why their grades are higher! Finally, are teachers better? Well, we can certainly argue that certain *aspects* of teaching have changed, and *some* of those changes are for the better, but that really isn't saying the same thing as 'teachers are better'. Therefore, our multivariate explanation for grade inflation cuts no mustard, because it is based on three unevidenced claims.

So what exactly is going on? I don't know for sure, of course. We must try to stick to the facts, however. It is true that the curriculum has changed, and true that the nature of the assessments and the marking system has changed. So, people are now taught different things, and marked in different ways, and the marks needed to achieve specific grades are now different. For example, there has been an increasing reliance on coursework, which increases the possibility that some people could cheat. I wouldn't suggest that this explains a lot of the grade inflation, but it might factor into the equation a little.

Comparisons with the past are probably impossible to make, and equally unfair on all concerned, so it is extremely difficult to conduct what on the surface is the obvious experiment: a direct comparison of scores obtained by students sitting both modern exams and those from 30 years ago.

Therefore, all we have is the knowledge that certain aspects of teaching have changed, the assessment system is different and the fact that grades have increased. We could argue forever about this. However, let us come back to a fundamental issue: what is the point of a public examination system? That surely must be to discriminate between people. That is, we use a standard examination so that we can work out which people are the best at something, which the worst and so on. If that isn't what it is for, it's very difficult to see its purpose. Therefore, we have a system that allows universities and employers to rank people and take the very best they can. It therefore doesn't matter one little bit whether grades are inflating or standards dropping, because the best are always the best and there will always be some people scoring lower. However, if more and more people achieve the highest grades, there is then no point in maintaining the system.

Let us imagine a system in which only the top 10 per cent of students achieve an 'A' grade. Imagine also that I have 10 jobs to allocate, and I have applications from 100 people. Of those, 10 will have achieved 'A' grades. However, in a system such as that which we have now, in which around 25 per cent are achieving that grade, I won't be able to easily tell the difference between 25 of my applicants. How do I pick the top ten? Furthermore, if trends of grade inflation increase, we can expect half of all candidates to achieve an 'A' grade in each examination in another 30 years! In less than a century, everyone might achieve an 'A'. You can no doubt imagine what the employer or university admissions officer is going to make of that!

The solution proposed is to create an 'A-star' grade, higher than 'A'. But how long will it be before a quarter of people sitting the examination achieve that grade, and also, why not just scale down the marking system and remove the need for a new grade? The marking scale needs to be a relative one, so you can move the grading anywhere you like. Of course, whether you mark more harshly, or you add a new grade, this only would work if there were a range of performance in the examination. If everyone gets everything right, which could happen in theory, then shifting the grading around makes no difference. In that case, the examiners would really have no option but to change the questions asked so that a proportion of people do badly. After all, as we have identified, the purpose of the system is *not* to give people medals for achievement, nor is it to reward hard work *per se*, but to allow us to find out who is better at particular subjects. Therefore, buried under all the political argument and debate about our education system is an underpinning question that we must address: is the system fit for its purpose? Nothing else actually matters. It was critical thinking that led us to realise that.

# UNIVERSITY LEAGUE TABLES

If you are reading this you are probably either at university or thinking of going to one soon: this maybe captures 90 per cent of the readership. In that case, you have probably looked at the various league tables of universities, perhaps to compare institutions. There's nothing more relevant to a psychologist than a critical evaluation of those kinds of statistics. The first thing you should note is that different league tables place universities at different points in their rankings. That lack of overall consistency should ring some alarm bells. If the tables were a valid indicator of university status, then they should mostly agree, but they don't.

It's true that the ones at the bottom tend to be near the bottom on all the tables. However, that's just about where the consistency ends. When you look at the fine detail, it all breaks down. The tables have various elements in them (we would call them *variables*), including research rating, teaching rating, student satisfaction and the like. Each of these is problematic in terms of how it can be assessed. Universities have pockets of excellence (and vice versa), so even if a university is generally rated low on research, the course you might be interested in could be in a department in which research was of international standing. Furthermore, a university that is foremost for research isn't necessarily so important to the average undergraduate student. They simply want to make sure that they will be taught properly, by qualified people, who they can see when they need to, and so on.

Equally, teaching excellence can be decided on the basis of qualifications of staff, ratings given by external agencies, student ratings, contributions to teaching literature and conferences, innovation in approach to curriculum and course design, and a number of other things. It's not simple.

Student satisfaction league tables are possibly those that potential students turn to most. After all, why not make your choice based on customer recommendations? It's what you'd do when you buy other things, so why not when buying an education? In theory that makes sense, but yet again you have to seriously wonder if you can trust the satisfaction surveys. Firstly, the sample sizes are relatively small. Compared to the many students in higher education, only a fraction of them bother to fill in the national surveys, and they tend to be those that are motivated to do so. Thus, the samples could easily be biased. Furthermore, it is in the interests of the students at an institution to make it sound good, because they don't want to leave with a degree from a university that is scuttling around at the bottom of the league tables. Also, you might be interested in applying to a department that is actually wonderful, but the overall rating of the university is lowered by some less good departments. It doesn't matter to you how good the Physics department is if you want to study Biology or French Literature.

On what basis is 'satisfaction' measured? We have the usual problem of it meaning different things to different people, and the issues around uses of attitude statements and Likert scales to determine satisfaction. We all know those arguments. Research methods books are full of them. If you ask someone 'How satisfied are you with library provision?' and expect them all to think the question means the same thing, you're in for a shock. Book stock, journal stock, electronic access, opening hours, library staff knowledge, helpfulness, toilet cleanliness? We could go on . . .

We should also consider issues such as reputation. In fact there is a very ironic relationship between reputation and satisfaction, which means that the league tables themselves can actually *move* universities up and down them. Let us say that the University of Brillingtonburyness has an excellent reputation; in fact it has been in the top ten for the last ten years. Students hear of this, and so choose to go there, with high expectations. We all know that hype is often difficult to live up to. So the students have unrealistically high expectations of the land of milk and honey they expect to find when they turn up at Brillingtonburyness, and they are a bit surprised to find that the library isn't papered with gold leaf and the lecturers aren't all geniuses and beautiful. It's good, but not that good. So they reflect that in their satisfaction ratings, pushing the institution down for years to come! Of course, that effect also can work the other way. If the University of Cratchington has a reputation for not being very good, and when you get there it seems ok or even quite good to you, then you push it up the table when you report on it.

Finally (although there are hundreds of points that can be made on this subject), let us consider what the relative positions in a league table mean. In the UK there are well over a hundred relevant institutions. When we average over various scales and scores we experience the issue of 'regression towards the mean': the more things you measure, the more everywhere looks pretty average, because high scores and low scores all start to even out. Only if a university is truly excellent or truly dire across every rating does this not happen. Next, scores are given based on averages across many students' satisfaction ratings. We therefore end up with decimal points that don't mean very much. If we use five-point Likert scales, for example, imagine the scores for satisfaction across five domains from ten people are as shown in the table below:

| | Library | Sports facilities | Catering and entertainment | Teaching | Courses |
|---|---|---|---|---|---|
| | 3 | 4 | 1 | 4 | 2 |
| | 2 | 3 | 1 | 4 | 2 |
| | 3 | 2 | 1 | 4 | 5 |
| | 5 | 3 | 1 | 4 | 2 |
| | 1 | 2 | 3 | 2 | 3 |
| | 3 | 3 | 5 | 2 | 1 |
| | 2 | 3 | 2 | 4 | 2 |
| | 4 | 3 | 4 | 3 | 1 |
| | 3 | 3 | 2 | 2 | 3 |
| | 1 | 4 | 2 | 3 | 2 |
| **Mean** | 2.7 | 2.8 | 2.2 | 3.2 | 2.3 |

We end up with the means shown at the bottom of the table. Based on a five-point Likert scale, what do those means indicate? If you then average all the means to get a total score, you end up with 2.64. Where is .64 of the distance between 2 and 3 on the scale you started with? It doesn't exist.

You might ask why this matters. A lot of the places in the league tables are just tiny fractions apart in scoring. Overall, the difference between one university and the next can be as little as 0.1 of a point across a scale that, if it uses total scores, say from 1 to 5 for 20 questions, can vary from 20 to 100, for example. This means that a university can jump 20 places in the league table by a tiny increase in its rating, averaged across a range of factors, and from a small percentage of the students attending the university. The tables can only really mean anything if you divide them into quartiles and make your decisions based on those alone. So, the top 25 per cent are probably very good, the next 25 per cent a bit worse, the next 25 per cent worse still, and the bottom 25 per cent might be the worst of all. Try to extract any finer detail than that and you are deluding yourself if you think it means much. Also, please do not forget that if you arbitrarily divide into quartiles, then those around their borders (for example the bottom of the first quartile and the top of the next) are really only tiny percentage points apart.

The moral of the tale is a simple one: league tables tell you very roughly who is good at certain things and who isn't – perhaps. Don't assume that two universities thirty places apart would be noticeably any different when you actually attend them, and don't assume that the top is unequivocally the best, or that the bottom is the worst. Finally, don't assume that the overall score for a university tells you much about the department in which you will be studying.

All of this is likely to make you wonder why we have league tables at all.

# REFLECTION AND CRITICAL THINKING

People in various professions, and students and trainees too, increasingly are being asked to reflect on their performance and skills. Many people find this particularly difficult, but in fact this is merely the application of critical thinking to the self, rather than the outside world. It is probably the only scenario in which we are required to do this. The most common problem is where people pass off a description of their thoughts and feelings as reflection. This is, in fact, necessary, but it is only the first stage of the legitimate reflection process.

*My manager suggested that I needed to prioritise my tasks better.*
*This made me very upset, and I was angry with her.*

This is a description, nothing more. There is no true reflection, because there is no critical thinking. Socratic questioning is useful here. Why is this upsetting? Is the emotional response justified? Is there a range of interpretations? What does my reaction tell me about myself? All of these types of questions must be asked, and if you can answer them, you've cracked reflection. All you then need to add is your solutions for similar situations in future, so that you develop and learn from your experiences. It really is that simple, but very difficult for some people who aren't trained to think this way.

---

## CHAPTER 3 – CRITICAL QUESTIONS

1. Using the examples in this chapter as a guide, think of an area of everyday life that you can dissect using critical thinking. Write a short essay doing just that.
2. What kind of art do you like? Examine why, and imagine how you would respond to someone who told you that it was 'rubbish'.

# 4 Critical Thinking Inside Psychology

## SYSTEMATIC REVIEWS

You might never have thought that systematic reviews are an exercise in critical thinking, but they are. In order to conduct a systematic review you have to make decisions about research you've read. It isn't a value-free process; in fact, systematic review is one of the most judgemental things psychologists will find themselves doing. However, judgemental doesn't mean 'prejudiced'. It's fine to set a predetermined set of criteria about what constitutes 'quality' and use that to decide which of a set of articles are worth including in a review and which are not. Other people can see the decisions you make, and choose to agree or disagree with you. Your list of criteria for inclusion in a systematic review, and your scale for judging the quality of each study, are both elements of the application of critical thinking, in particular in a research context. If psychologists don't apply critical thinking in research, they end up believing the results of badly conducted studies, and conducting their own studies in a shoddy fashion too.

Most of the criteria for judging study quality come 'off the shelf': stock criticisms, as it were. We have to ask if the studies have adequate power, if the samples are made up correctly, if the design allows a proper comparison between treatment and control, if the analysis is correct and so on. In addition, each individual area for systematic review brings its own questions about the research. In combination, the two make for a robust critical exercise. Don't forget, also, that when it isn't possible to do a systematic review – for example when the research on a topic is too diverse – we often conduct a *critical review* instead. The lowest level of criticality comes in the form of a literature review, which doesn't necessarily make value judgements about the research at all, or at least makes use of a wide range of research of varying quality. It is, arguably, more *descriptive* than critical.

# CRITICAL THINKING IN STATISTICS AND PROBABILITY

Have you ever been struck by what appears to be a string of remarkable coincidences? Are you the kind of person who senses meaning in such coincidences, perhaps the intervention of something supernatural? Let us take a typical example or two. After that, we'll try to apply ourselves to something psychological.

Nostradamus was a famous French apothecary and visionary. According to some, he *predicted* a range of things that happened hundreds of years after his death, including World War II and the rise of Adolf Hitler. His key predictions date back to a publication in 1555 in which he refers to events in rather vague terms, and often gets things slightly wrong. Of course, 'slightly wrong' is just plain wrong. You can't claim the lottery jackpot prize if your numbers are all one digit away from the winning numbers. But when Nostradamus and others like him are one number out, we assume it's spooky and supernatural. He doesn't actually refer to Hitler, for example: he specifically names 'Hister'.

Century 2, Quatrain 24, in one translation, can be rendered in this way:

*Beasts ferocious with hunger will cross the rivers,*
*The greater part of the battlefield will be against Hister.*
*Into a cage of iron will the great one be drawn,*
*When the child of Germany observes nothing.*

So, that's quite near, yes? Except for the fact that scholars tell us that 'Hister' is the Latin name for the Danube: it has nothing to do with the German dictator. What are the beasts ferocious with hunger? What is the cage of iron? Why does Germany have a child and why does it observe nothing? There is only one thing here that really is anything close to a prediction of the war, and even that is wrong. Also, the original French refers to 'Germain', not Germany. This isn't the modern-day Germany, but an old area known as Germania, which only loosely maps onto the Germany of Hitler. If you need further convincing, and you know any French, remember that Germain still exists as a French word in place names like St Germain, but the French name for Germany is *Allemagne*. This word comes from the Alamanni tribe. But here's the odd part: they lived around the Rhine, not the Danube (Hister). Nostradamus simply can't seem to match anything up at all.

There are also various competing translations of Nostradamus' work. Each one is closer or further away from a real event, depending how you look at it. Furthermore, Nostradamus made many, many prophecies. Most seem to bear no relation to actual events, no matter how hard we try to make them (and there are many thousands of people doing their level best to make them fit). So what Nostradamus did is say a lot of very vague things. Some of those vague things match up a bit with some real events. But never once did he make a specific, verifiable prediction. Nostradamus never said things like 'In 2009, a man named Barack will become leader of the most powerful nation, replacing a man from a family rich from oil whose father stood before him'. *That* would be impressive.

The final thing to remember about this is that we always use hindsight to check his prophecies. No one ever reads Nostradamus and accurately states that a certain event will occur in a specific way at a specific time. Instead, we wait for things to happen, then find something in what Nostradamus wrote which turns out to be true. This is called *postdiction*. In statistics, it is the equivalent of collecting data, then analysing it, and then writing a hypothesis to fit what you've discovered: it breaks all the rules of scientific endeavour. Furthermore, if you collect enough data you are bound to find something you can comment on. We call this *data mining*. We also refer to this kind of situation as *post-hockery*. It's why we have the notion of correction for family-wise errors in statistics. You can't just run twenty t-tests with an alpha value of 5 per cent, .05 or 1/20. Each one of the tests has that value, which means that in a set of 20, one of them will look significant by chance alone! Furthermore, you won't know which one it is, rendering all of them dubious. What we do is adjust the alpha, so that a difference has to be very, very unlikely to occur by chance for us to accept it. Instead of 5 per cent error, we go for 0.25 per cent error instead, for example. If we applied this to Nostradamus, given the thousands of prophecies, we would end up saying that in order to accept a prophecy, we would have to have some of them *exactly* right. There isn't a single prophecy like this.

I like the odds on being right eventually if you hedge your bets. In fact, I'm going to do the same. Here are my prophecies, and watch out for them in the next 500 years. In fact, I'd go so far as to say that *some* of these will 'come true' within ten years.

- There will be a great taking over of green.
- Crab-men will resist until the sands are blackened.
- A woman from the north will separate father from child, and her name will be Therese.
- Men will stop in their tracks with a mighty disease that makes sounds.
- A machine will decide our names and no one shall carry the Great Three over the river.

What I have just done here is the equivalent of setting a hypothesis like this:

---

There will be a significant difference between scores obtained from participants in the two conditions, or there won't. At some point, we might find one, although it might look like something else.

---

Around a decade ago the internet first got wind of a forum poster, 'TimeTravel_0', who eventually revealed himself to be one John Titor, who made various predictions about the future. Titor claimed to be an American soldier and a time traveller from the year 2036. You can investigate this rather unusual phenomenon yourself, since the internet has no shortage of pages and information about John, who disappeared as mysteriously as he appeared. Many of his predictions didn't happen, but the beauty of the argument is that John explained that his predictions might be wrong in our world, because the many-worlds theory in quantum mechanics was actually correct. This means that in his world something did happen, but it isn't necessarily the same version of our world that he has travelled back into. Confused? Well, the theory is that there are infinite universes, where anything and everything happens. We are only living in one of them, but the others are all 'here' somewhere, right next to this one, perhaps only a millionth of an inch away, but inaccessible to us. If John managed to come from one version of our world into another one, not everything he saw happen in his world would happen in ours.

Of course, this begs two questions. Firstly, how did he get his universes mixed up to end up in this one, and secondly, did he ever get back to his? Hoax or not (and we can't be sure that it is or isn't a hoax), John Titor is like a modern-day Nostradamus, except he wasn't making predictions, but telling us what is yet to happen in our world, and he supplied details about the time machine he used to travel in. It is fascinating stuff, regardless of the truth of the matter.

# THE TEXAS SHARPSHOOTER FALLACY

A man in Texas fires random shots at a barn wall, then paints targets over the holes. His neighbours see the products of his labours, and he looks like a sharpshooter. Can you predict what this section of the book is about?

Fitting hypotheses to data that already exist is a dangerous process; you are putting the cart before the horse. The Texan *looks* like a sharpshooter, but that doesn't mean that he is. Nostradamus is like the Texan who shoots, and in the modern world the supporters of Nostradamus are painting the targets around the holes for him.

If you have ever wondered why we need a scientific approach to discovery of the world's secrets, including hypothesis testing, rather than simply observation, the **Texas sharpshooter fallacy** demonstrates it. If all we do is to look at what is already there and try to fit theories around it, we end up in trouble.

Let's play join the dots (American readers will know this as 'connect the dots').

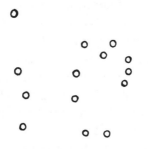

Now, we could join these dots like this:

Or, this would be fine too:

Which is correct? Well, they both are, and yet neither is. Fitting lines (theories) to dots (observations) often tells us only about our personal preferences for shapes, not about the true nature of the connections of the dots. Good science is conducted by first drawing a series of lines, then suggesting that the dots will be at specific positions. Then we reveal the dots and see if we were correct. Or, we observe dot patterns, then we build lines between them, and then we test the theory we used to join the dots by seeing how many dot patterns that theory helps us to join up. If it works over and over again, with different configurations of dots, we are probably onto something. Without hypothesis and test, we simply get stuck saying 'there are multiple truths', which is philosophically very interesting, but doesn't get bridges built or satellites positioned.

# THE GAMBLER'S FALLACY, THE CLUSTERING ILLUSION, APOPHENIA, PAREIDOLIA AND OTHER WONDERFUL THINGS

Fundamentally, human beings have some excellent cognitive abilities. We can solve problems, perceive things, ponder, talk, add up numbers, invent things and so on. However, because our brains have developed to work in particular ways that are very useful to us most of the time, we are also suckers for a con trick – and many con tricks exist in nature, or emerge from it.

Our world consists of 'stuff'. Lots and lots of stuff, floating around, stuck together, expanding, contracting, moving, leaving, returning, sparkling, exploding, bright, dull, coloured, noisy, tinkling, buzzing, smelly and so on. Just stop for a moment and look around you. Try to look at everything as separate bits of stimulation. The wall in front of you isn't a wall. Try to see it as a patch of something, with stuff on it. The table isn't a table, but some stuff perched on some other stuff that appears bigger at the front (remember that perspective is not present in the object: you make it happen). Look at a face. It isn't a face, but shapes moving around in relation to other shapes.

You could not function like that without distress; it would be like a very severe form of perceptual problem. So your brain does millions of calculations at lightning speed, shaping and transforming the world into things that make sense for you, that enable you to get on with daily life without being bombarded with stimuli. Your brain throws most things 'out of focus', leaving only the things you need in focus at any given time, and it clusters things together, so we perceive a face, a table, a wall.

Isn't that wonderful? Yes, it is, but it's also a big problem when it comes to critical thinking, because we have evolved an overwhelming need, which we really can't switch off, to search for *patterns* in things.

We extract meaning. The trouble is that some things aren't meaningful at all: some things out there really are random. Our perceptual systems just cannot cope easily with that idea. We resist randomness, and we struggle when trying consciously to switch off the search for patterns and meaning in data.

**Apophenia** is a word used to describe the phenomenon whereby we see meaningful patterns in random data or stimuli. Shermer (2008) calls it 'patternicity', although I think that 'apophenia' is a much more interesting word. **Pareidolia** is much the same thing, but is used to describe the brain's tendency to find patterns in noise, usually visual or auditory. So apophenia could be used to describe situations in which people develop conspiracy theories by searching for patterns in higher-order events ('adding two and two together to make five', as people say), whereas pareidolia is reserved for lower-order perceptual phenomena. When we see faces in clouds, or we hear a telephone when we're in the shower, that's pareidolia. Our mind constantly hunts for recognisable things in the world in front of us, so powerfully that it invents things that aren't there. The evidence of your senses is truly not good evidence at all.

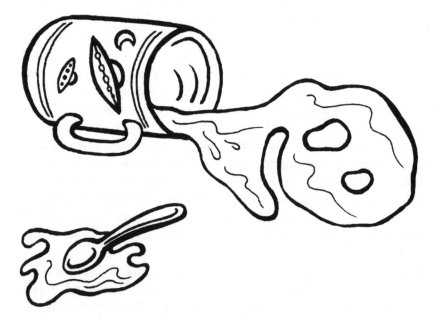

When you are given an argument that picks out facts and strings them together, you have a natural tendency to accept it. Critical thinking is all about being vigilant. You must be aware that because something *seems like* a good idea, it might be nothing more than a chance cluster of facts. When you think you see a pattern in your data, you might actually be inventing it.

The **clustering illusion** is basically the apparent meaningfulness in clusters of events. It occurs partly because most people have an aversion to randomness, and struggle to comprehend the fact that random things display patterns, but that those patterns are utterly devoid of meaning or intentionality. The clustering illusion can cause us to really think something is happening and to start to build theories on it. When we conduct research and subject our data to a statistical analysis, we mostly take the clustering illusion out of the frame. Our statistical tests are designed to look for trends in data that are likely, and unlikely, as it were. Our tests help us to reject things which are likely to occur by chance alone, leaving us with a probability of that happening, which we interpret. A $p$ value of $< .05$ tells us that the 'trend' or 'cluster' of events we have observed would happen by chance less than one time in twenty. It *could* happen by chance, but it isn't likely. So a cluster might be unlikely, and the more consistent or large the cluster, the less likely it is. However, it is still possible.

A bigger problem occurs when we get clusters in qualitative studies. Here we have no statistical benchmark against which to judge the findings. Therefore, what can happen is that a random cluster can look like a meaningful pattern in discourse, or a 'theme' emerging, when it's just chance. There's nothing to stop a qualitative researcher from getting carried away because something keeps jumping out of the data – apart from their own common sense and training, of course.

The **gambler's fallacy** – the feeling that if you play long enough, you will eventually win – is almost like the opposite of the clustering illusion, but is underpinned by a similar issue: the failure to grasp randomness. This is the thing that makes gambling so addictive. Quite simply, it feels, very strongly, as if perseverance will pay. Unfortunately it doesn't. It isn't true, and all the figures show that. However, the feeling that you will eventually win is overwhelming for some people. The odds of winning a lottery are millions to one, but people feel that if they keep playing they will eventually win. They almost certainly won't. In fact, if the odds of winning are 1 in 14 million, and they are the same *every time you play*. Playing week after week doesn't change that. Also (and here's the cruel part), the odds remain the same even for people who have won. That's right: if you win a major prize, you still have exactly the same chance of winning it the week after, and the week after that, and so on. However, something in the human psyche feels that all this can't be true. If we didn't have this feeling, gambling would not be addictive, nor would it exist as an industry.

We have digressed a little, so I should remind you why I took the discussion down this path: it is important to stand back from your own feelings sometimes. Human nature, and human perception, are somewhat flawed. Now and then we need to try to switch off our feelings and focus on the facts. This is crucial to critical thinking, even though I urge you not to completely forget your feelings. Sometimes your feelings are your 'moral compass' that keeps your critical thinking in check.

# PSEUDOSCIENCE AND THE ENEMIES OF PSYCHOLOGY

We have come this far and it is time to take a lot of what we've learned and apply it. We know what science is, hopefully, and we know how to think more critically. We should now be able to put two and two together and examine **pseudoscience**. The first thing we need to do is be aware that pseudoscience is false science, and until we gather facts we cannot properly distinguish between it and what is often called **protoscience**, which is basically science in infancy. When people first dream their dreams about how the world might work, they create theories that can sometimes predate the methods we need to test them. That's protoscience, potentially. The difficulty is that until something is evidenced, it isn't science; it remains pseudoscience. So, we have to stick with that term. Apologies will be due to anything that we end up criticising that turns out later to have been genuine protoscience – that is, science in the making. We just aren't in a position to know right now.

Pseudoscience is characterised in a number of ways. Some of these characteristics are shared with science, but curiously some of them are the opposite of what science is and does.

## *Jargon*

Real science needs jargon. It might be an annoyance to students, but we do actually need it so that scientists can talk to each other. It's not just science that has jargon: the arts do too, and many hobbies. Pseudoscience often has just as much jargon as real science. Of course, the lay public would be forgiven for being sucked in by this. On the surface, all those fancy words make pseudoscience look indistinguishable from the real thing. What makes this even worse is that one subtle characteristic of the use of jargon (and ideas) in pseudoscience is the misappropriation of proper scientific terms. What pseudoscientists commonly do is use their own special words, but also those from science too, albeit in the wrong way. This makes it even more difficult for people to tell the two apart. A lot of 'New Age' theories about the universe borrow ideas and terms from quantum physics. However, just because there are weird and wonderful ideas that make sense when you are describing the properties of subatomic particles does not mean that the same things apply to human beings. Yes, electrons can spin clockwise and anticlockwise at the same time. That doesn't mean that it's happening to you. Nor does it mean that you can hold entirely contradictory beliefs and use quantum mechanics to excuse yourself!

There certainly is a way in which a particle can be twinned with another particle, such that altering one changes the other, even when they are millions of light years apart. This is called *quantum entanglement*. But it doesn't mean that you have a soul mate. Nor does it mean that you can have telepathic contact with beings on other planets if only you could find a way to communicate. In the many-worlds interpretation there are other universes 'vibrating' just next to ours, and it just so happens that we are only tuned in to ours, missing all the rest, but that doesn't mean that you can visit other universes by changing your vibrational resonance and 'popping across' for a trip.

In psychology we know that different personality types exist, but it doesn't follow that you can change yours easily, or that yours is determined by the moon. From jargon, it's a small step to misuse of ideas: the two are very neatly linked together.

A long-standing and recurring joke amongst chemistry students and the like which has found its way into popular life concerns a bit of jargon. There is a chemical called dihydrogen monoxide, or sometimes 'hydroxylic acid', which is present in much of the food we eat and in all sorts of other common objects. It can be fatal if inhaled. It is corrosive, and is a major component of acid rain. Objects remain contaminated with it even after washing. However, our politicians don't seem to care. There is a big industry dealing with dihydrogen monoxide and the money seems to blind people to the dangers of it. I should point out, if you haven't guessed, that 'dihydrogen monoxide' is *water*. Jargon has a lot to answer for.

## Training

Scientists spend a long time training. It varies from country to country, but the basic training for a scientist is an undergraduate degree, possibly an MSc, then a doctorate, and maybe more beyond that. This takes between six and twelve years, depending on the system you are in. In pseudoscience, it's just the same. People have to learn their trade in just the same way, although sometimes you do wonder what they are actually learning, given that at the end of it they don't always seem to know anything that is of any use, except about making money.

A long training is necessary in the sciences, because there is a lot to learn. A long training in pseudosciences is, arguably, nothing more than a way to make what is done seem clever. It is very difficult to give you concrete examples of this, because quite a few pseudoscientists like suing people who criticise them. I certainly don't have the money behind me to get into a protracted Court case. However, if you dig around the internet you'll find what I'm talking about: people and organisations that lay claim to being able to solve all sorts of problems – fad diets are sometimes an example – with little or no genuine science behind them, but a lot of terminology, 'experience' and arguments picked from science in a very unsystematic way.

## Secrecy and mystery

Unlike science, which tries to be transparent and public, a lot of pseudoscience loses its cachet if it loses its mystery. Some pseudoscientists avoid being subjected to any form of scrutiny, and do their very best to get out of explaining anything in all but the vaguest of terms. Scientists say 'Here's what I think: attack it'. That is how science proceeds. Pseudoscience rarely does this. Normally, you'll hear a pseudoscientist saying things like 'You can't use normal methods to analyse what I do', and 'There's more to life than science and its methods'. You can't win with these people. Imagine the bizarre arguments that would occur between a scientist and a pseudoscientist if both of them used the defences of mystery. It would sound like two children debating in the playground:

*'I know something you don't know.'*
*'So what? I know you're wrong.'*
*'Well, there's something else I know but I can't tell you that means I am right, so there.'*
*'Well, you would not understand what I know, it takes training, but I am right.'*

This could go on for some time. A real scientist should be open and say clearly what they believe and why they believe it. They invite scrutiny and criticism, and they welcome change. Be very wary of anyone selling you a theory that isn't abiding by these principles.

## Stasis

Pseudoscience is in sharp contrast with science in that it seems largely static. It rarely shows any signs of progress over time, while real science changes all the time. We collect evidence and we change our minds based on it. Pseudoscience starts with a theory and sticks with it. Sometimes, pseudoscientists argue that the reason that they don't change is because X many years ago discovered a 'universal truth'.

## Psychology as a protoscience

Now you know what the characteristics of pseudoscience are, you might like to reflect on where psychology is and how far down the road from protoscience to science we actually are. Naturally, this isn't an easy question, for various reasons. A number of philosophers of science and qualitative researchers would say that we are not even travelling on the road to science at all, and they might even question the value of that particular path anyway. But, if you accept for a moment that many psychologists do want to be regarded as scientists, then you might wish to think about psychology's history, and whether we are yet in a position to try to assess where we are.

If you use the criteria above, then we seem to be quite a way down the road. We have a necessary training (as opposed to an unnecessary one for pseudoscience), and we have jargon – lots of it. We have evidence that our theories change over time in the light of evidence, so we are not static. We certainly don't wish to be mystical or secretive. There's a big push in the UK to try to bring psychology to society, and to correct public misapprehensions about psychology. We wouldn't be doing that if we wanted to look like magicians. In fact, we are long way from what sceptics tend to call 'woo-woo'. Woo-woo, or sometimes just 'woo', is the term for nonsense posing as science.

There is a continuum from superstition to mature science that passes through pseudoscience, then *fringe science*, then protoscience. The question should really be whether psychology is a fringe science or a protoscience. The philosopher Schopenhauer said that truth passes through stages: the first ridicule, the second opposition and the third acceptance as common sense. Fringe science belongs somewhere in the 'ridiculous' category, verging towards opposition. Psychology seems to inherit an interesting sliding position, moving back and forth between all three of Schopenhauer's stages, depending on the area of psychology involved. For example, some of our most concrete findings about memory belong firmly in the 'accepted' camp, while some of our work in the qualitative arena is still strongly opposed, while finally we have the ridiculed work. There isn't much of this, but it does exist, albeit rarely published (perhaps because it is ridiculed?). Some of the earlier work in parapsychology suffered in this way. What is interesting about psychology is the fact that it isn't a monolithic subject, but a massive, widespread area of endeavour, which means it is especially difficult to characterise or pin down.

That said, it is worth thinking about those so-called elements of psychology that aren't really psychological at all, but which purport to be. What follows is a discussion of three of these.

## Three enemies of psychology

There are more than three, but I'd like to focus here on three big enemies of psychology. Why 'enemies'? Because they set themselves up like psychology, they borrow from psychology and the public confuse them with real psychology. If we, as psychologists, are going to become angry and protest, perhaps we should start with these: astrology, graphology and phrenology.

## Astrology

Astrology is a collective term for a range of practices in which human behaviour is 'explained' by reference to planetary positions and movements, and even where events are 'predicted'. Astrology covers Western, Indian and Chinese forms, and there are many variants of each. For the purposes of argument, we will focus only on the Western form here, which is centred around twelve basic 'signs' (the Zodiac) and the relationship between personality and when a person was born. In its simplest form, and that which is mostly easily discredited, *when* you are born places you within one of the signs, and each sign is associated with various characteristics and traits. Some astrologers deny that this is meaningful in any way, but it is the form in which the horoscopes in our magazines and newspapers are presented. People in their hundreds of thousands, millions across the world, read their daily horoscopes, believing to a lesser or greater extent that these are some kind of prediction of their day or week ahead.

Firstly, it seems strange to suggest that one twelfth of the population of the world have one set of characteristics, another twelve a different set, and so on. (I know that the population doesn't divide up equally into twelves because there are clusters in certain months, but bear with me, since there are still millions upon millions of people with birthdays in each month of the year.) It simply doesn't seem to add up. In fact, it is a short stretch from that to suggesting that there are only twelve basic kinds of people.

The next problem is the idea that your personality would be dictated fairly precisely by when in a year you are born. There seems to be no *mechanism* for that. It might be possible that early experiences dictate certain aspects of personality, and being born in the hot weather or cold weather might make a difference, at least theoretically, but that's about as far as logic can take us. Even that is problematic, since basic horoscopes don't seem to suggest that they are based on geography, and not all people live in parts of the world with actual seasons: on the equator it's the same weather all year round, pretty much. Furthermore, the personality characteristics that are suggested by some astrologers are entirely untested. When I say 'untested', I should point out that there have been studies into the extent to which people identify with the characteristics associated with the Zodiac signs. Those show, time after time, that there is no relationship between true personality and those characteristics claimed, except that almost everybody finds something true about themselves in every single Zodiac sign, rendering that level of operation useless.

If we all show elements of all signs, how can the Zodiac be substantiated? There are failings of logic left, right and centre here. The way that the characteristics are set out means that they can easily apply to anyone. Commonly, Zodiac sign descriptions are vague or even contradictory. 'You are calm, but now and then you have trouble keeping your temper'. Isn't that almost everyone? 'You are tough but with a softer side'. 'You are a softie, but with a tougher side'. 'You like to please people'. 'You sometimes doubt yourself'. Can you see anything here that doesn't describe 99 per cent of people on Earth?

Of course, this is the simple, cheap and easy version of astrology. More complicated versions abound, and they focus on very specific issues around exact place and time of birth, although many people don't have this information – I have met people from some countries in Africa who for cultural reasons do not know how old they are, let alone their time of birth – and the alignment of the planets at this time. Of course, they cannot be the same for everyone on Earth, including those born at exactly the same time as you, since you don't share the specific *place* of birth with them, just the time. The problem remains, however, that there is no postulated system for explaining why this would either determine someone's personality or indeed imply what their future would hold. In addition, not only is no system of cause and effect put forward that makes any sense in the physical world, there is also no clear way of working out how some people know this and some don't. You can only learn something concrete: you can't learn something that isn't defined and written down for all to see. Instead, astrologists refer to 'tapping into cosmic forces' and the like, which simply moves the problem around rather than solves it. Which forces? How do they work? How do those forces alter or shape people? Magically, it seems.

All of this may seem irrelevant were it not for the fact that astrologers are effectively trying to do the job of psychologists without any of the training, the scientific rigour or the transparency. It is our job to describe personality and understand the formation of it. We do it because we want to understand human behaviour and, at times, model or predict who will do what, when and why. For astrologers to suggest that they can do this can seem like an insult to the trained psychologists working in the field of personality.

### *Graphology*
Graphology makes another largely unverified series of claims around the idea that handwriting reveals something about the character of the writer. In its most simple form there is more of a plausible idea behind graphology than that behind astrology. Your hand movements are controlled by your central nervous system. It is the brain that is also responsible for you being who you are. Therefore, it might be possible that that which determines your personality also expresses itself in

your movements, including the way you write things. A very meticulous person probably writes quite neatly, for example. Unfortunately, that's where the potential sense and reason stops, in my opinion and in that most of the scientists who have studied this field.

From that point on, though, things are considerably more nebulous. Different 'schools' of graphology have entirely different and contrasting ideas, which is a bit like having eight different chemistries working in parallel. Imagine incompatible versions of chemistry, each claiming to explain the properties of physical substances, each having very little evidence of any kind to support it. When graphologists are put to the test they are very rarely successful. The best test, perhaps, is to predict accurately the personality characteristics of someone you have never met purely from their handwriting. Unfortunately, when this is done, it tends to take the form of making the kind of statements that astrologers make, which are non-scientific, non-psychological, and apply to most people. 'I can see from the handwriting that this is a person who takes pride in their work, but can be lazy at times. They probably like the outdoors, but not necessarily mountain climbing or rambling, perhaps just gardening or walks in the city.' So it goes on: vague, catch-all statements, which do not pin their originator down in any way but which people feel are accurate, but are no better than chance.

It is very important to note, however, that graphologists should not be mistaken for forensic handwriting experts. These are people who genuinely can make a difference. They don't make predictions in a semi-supernatural way. Instead, they take samples of handwriting and compare them, to be able to declare with a specified level of accuracy the chances of both pieces coming from the same writer. They analyse pen strokes to determine if a signature is a forgery, for example. It isn't an exact science, but it follows scientific principles of measurement and comparison. These people are not graphologists, even though that word would etymologically suit them well. They are generally referred to as *forensic handwriting analysts* or *questioned document analysts*.

Psychologists should be aware of graphology because many of the schools of graphology borrow from psychology and psychoanalysis, and make claims about providing psychological insight. The training for graphologists (there isn't a single agreed training) involves some study of psychology, but not under the auspices of The British Psychological Society (BPS), the professional body for psychologists. This effectively means that the psychology studied by graphologists does not have to be regulated in the same way for its quality, the qualifications of those who teach it, or for any aspect of its quality assurance. I am not claiming that some graphology organisations don't have quality assurance mechanisms, but they don't have BPS quality assurance mechanisms. Ask yourself why universities offer psychology courses but tend not to offer graphology. If you are keen to pursue graphology as a course of study, ask the people offering the course what quality assurance measures they follow. Do they have, for example, an external examiner? Do they have double-marking procedures, course validation procedures, annual review and so on? I suspect many will have none of these key features of standard educational provision, yet they offer courses with a substantial psychology component in them.

There is a statement on a graphology website which says that there is empirical evidence (and they imply that this is psychological evidence) that a specific writing style is associated with a specific personality characteristic, and they state, quite categorically, that this is a link that occurs in all cases to some extent. There is no reference to any published research studies that back this up. I can see nothing to substantiate this claim whatever, except that someone said it. At least, the website doesn't give any research evidence, and I cannot find any evidence myself that would match up to the claim. I can't quote it specifically, simply because the law and science don't mix in a fair way. Firstly, I would have to seek permission to quote their words, and they might not grant it unless I was saying positive things about it. Secondly, criticising others' claims on seemingly perfectly rational scientific grounds isn't generally ok, and if your opponents' lawyers are good enough you can find yourself in hot water even if all you have done is point out a factual error.

It might seem strange to you, and not very sensible in terms of a critical thinking approach, but if you set yourself up as a 'Trumpologist', and I point out that there is no evidence that Trumpology works, you can sue me, and the fact that what I said isn't untrue doesn't mean a thing. You still might win. Compare this with a situation in which psychologists who are professionally registered can theoretically be struck off from practising for failing to keep good records, for example. The Trumpologist can say pretty much anything they like without reference to any body of knowledge that is recognised, and offer all kinds of services, and it's difficult to touch them. In contrast, the fully qualified psychologist treads across a metaphorical frozen lake all the time.

Most of the websites I visited refer to graphology somewhere in the text as the *science* of graphology.

### Phrenology

Phrenology is another approach that has lost popularity, but was all the rage a century or two ago. You've probably all seen a phrenology map drawn on a porcelain cranium – your place of study might have one in a cupboard somewhere. There was a time when these were popular, partly as tools to teach people how inappropriate some of the claims were, and partly from the days when faith was placed in phrenology, even amongst some scientists. For some reason, publishers' designers went through a phase lasting about thirty years during which they seemed obsessed with putting a picture of a phrenology head on the cover of textbooks of psychology. They did the same with the psi symbol for psychology. Sometimes the head was in silhouette, sometimes not. Have a look at the hundreds of psychology texts your library probably contains and see how many you can spot with a head on the cover!

Phrenology still exists, despite it being almost entirely dropped by psychologists a very long time ago, and it is still referred to as a science by many of those who stick with it today, despite there being virtually no conventional science attached to it. The original phrenologists *were* onto something, in that they recognised that different parts of the brain do different things. The next step in the logic does also have some credible evidence behind it: that people with different skills and abilities have developed various parts of their brain to different degrees, but then it starts to veer away from science. Phrenology is based on the premise that those variations in brain activity (or even brain size and development) manifest themselves in variation of the cranium or skull. So, if you are good at football, there will be a way of detecting that by palpating the skull. Needless to say, there is nothing in modern science that backs up this part of the theory, which essentially means we have to stop there. There is no clear mechanism for brain development affecting skull development, except in the most extreme cases, such as where a baby (whose skull has not hardened) has a profound untreated case of a condition such as hydrocephalus, which could distort the skull and cause it to form in an unusual way. This does not, however, mean that the child will have any special abilities corresponding to the area that is most prominent. In short, phrenology doesn't stand up to scrutiny.

# DISCOURSE ANALYSIS: A PRACTICAL APPLICATION OF CRITICAL THINKING

There is no unified definition of discourse analysis; it means a lot of things to a lot of people. However, regardless of the detail, it generally involves breaking down a text and identifying the types of language used, argument structures and devices that constitute the whole. In fact, the terms used by discourse analysts map onto those we might use to describe aspects of critical thinking.

One example is the *extreme case formulation*. This is where the speaker tries to back their own argument by recourse to its alleged commonness. For instance, 'Everybody likes a glass of wine.' Of course this is blatantly untrue, but we've all heard things like this, and have probably all said them, if not about wine. Another example might be 'We've all heard things like this, and have probably all said them.' In critical thinking, we call this the *ad populum* argument, but it's essentially the same thing. Recourse to the majority as a way of substantiating an opinion is effectively nothing more than a fallacy. Just because something is thought or done by most people does not make it right. Sometimes – in fact quite often – the minority is right.

# CRITICAL THINKING IN RESEARCH METHODS AND STATISTICS

Your critical thinking skills will pay dividends when it comes to research methods; it is often the people with the best critical skills who find this area of psychology relatively easy. Research methods as a subject is based entirely on logic, and applying logic is a fundamental part of critical thinking.

You need to think about why certain research designs are used and not others. The right design tells us things that the wrong design can't. That's a matter of logic, and a good critical thinker can identify the right and wrong designs easily. They can also work out if a theory is flawed depending on the nature of the data collected to support it, including how those data were collected.

When you write an essay, you use evidence from the research literature. Of course, the best essays make use of the evidence carefully, and analyse studies to look for flaws. This is especially important when you are writing a systematic review, which you will almost certainly do if you are or wish to become a postgraduate student or eventually a researcher in your own right.

## Correlation and causation

This is something you were taught early on. Because two things are correlated does not mean that one thing causes the other. You've probably been given hundreds of examples of this before, so I don't need to create yet more. Just look out for situations in which writers and researchers make the leap from correlation to theory based on causation.

Journalists commonly make this mistake when they write up research they have read about. For example, we know that parents who smoke are more likely to have delinquent children than parents who do not smoke. We also know that people who have dogs are healthier than cat owners. The obvious conclusions are that smoking parents cause delinquency in their children, and getting a dog will improve your health. Think of the alternative explanations that avoid this simple correlation-causation link.

## Control groups

Sometimes the lack of a control group can make a big difference to a research conclusion, or the wrong kind of control group can be used. The whole point of a control group is that there is a comparison between doing nothing and doing something. A control group should consist of the same people doing nothing, or a group of people who are almost entirely the same as the treatment group except for the fact that they are doing nothing. When controls don't match the treatment or experimental group, you've got a recipe for problems.

Very often researchers base their work on an *assumption* that their control group is to all intents and purposes comprised of the same kinds of people as the experimental group or groups, but they don't often test that assumption. If they do, it is often only on the basis of one or two characteristics like age and sex; they are relying on a statistical probability that their control group won't differ substantially from the other group. If you randomly allocate people to conditions, and the samples are large enough, then the chances of those conditions differing before you even do anything is small. It isn't zero, however.

Of course, this means that you should always think about the quality of control groups in terms of these issues. Are the samples suitably large, and were participants randomly assigned to conditions? If the answer to either of these is 'no', then you could be reading about flawed research. If the answer is 'no' to both questions, assume that you are.

## Blind and double-blind

We know that people have a tendency to do what they think you want them to do. We also know that researchers have a tendency to see things how they want to see them. Trying not to do this is like trying not to blink. You can do it for a while, but eventually, human nature kicks in whether you like it or not and whether you realise it or not. That's why we have created blind and double-blind procedures. If research participants don't know what group they are in, they can hardly react according to expectations, because they have none (blind). If you as the researcher also don't know, you won't interpret their behaviour in a way that suits you, nor will you subtly behave differently towards them (double blind).

It is not always possible to have double-blind procedures, and often you can't have blind procedures either, but researchers should do their best to minimise demand characteristics (demand characteristics are what the participant *thinks* the study is all about). Even if a participant knows what you are doing with them, it's best if they don't know what you are doing to the people in the other groups. That keeps them in the shadows, even if keeping them in the dark is impossible.

## Observation and interpretation

Always examine whether the conclusions drawn from data stand up to outside scrutiny. It's very easy for a researcher to see in data what they had hoped to see, but others might differ. This is especially true in the case of observational studies, in which the data naturally lend themselves to much inference and interpretation. Just because a child is bashing a toy against a wall doesn't mean it is frustrated or angry, but if the researcher believes it is, that will be the interpretation. In fact, it could be simply because the child wants attention, or because it likes the sound, or because it wants to make a hole in the wall, or break the toy to get another one.

Check to see whether the researchers have used multiple observers and coders, and preferably *independent* observers who have no idea what the researchers expect to find. You will often find that they have done the former but not the latter. Sometimes there are only two coders or raters, and they are the two researchers, both of whom were involved in setting up the study, recruiting participants, analysing data and so on. There's a stock, off-the-shelf criticism for you.

## History repeating itself

If you look at the work of a single researcher or group of researchers, you will sometimes find that previous works and interpretations of data are used to justify publishing the same interpretations again. Sometimes that amounts to little more than repeating previous mistakes. If a researcher makes an error, but manages to get it published, there's nothing to stop them using that published work to prop up more mistaken ideas in the future. There's something terribly flawed in an argument which says 'Previously, I suggested that X causes Y to happen. I now present to you more data, collected in slightly different circumstances, again showing a relationship between X and Y, which I wish to postulate is because X causes Y, precisely because I suggested that last time.' It really is a weak argument, but you'll find it.

## The wrong analysis

Look for incorrect analysis being performed. Sometimes, researchers report parametric inferential analyses when in fact the data are not best suited to that approach. Have the researchers made all the checks and balances required to identify that data are normally distributed, and so on? Are the scales of measurement used treated as if they yield ratio data, when in fact it is interval, or even ordinal? Do they have enough participants in each cell of an ANOVA analysis? Are they discussing a 'non-significant trend', which basically means nothing?

## *'Bigging up' weak results*

Look very carefully at results on which theories might be based. In particular, pay attention to correlation and regression. Don't just accept correlations because they are statistically significant. There's a big difference between significant and *meaningful*, and we'll explore this again in the next section. A small correlation might be statistically significant, but very unimpressive and showing a fairly unclear relationship between variables. If you have a big enough sample size, correlations of .3 can be 'highly significant', but are still weak.

Look also at regression models. Look at the adjusted $r^2$ that is reported (if it is reported at all). This takes into account the number of predictor variables in the regression. A 'significant model' can emerge, and the authors might be very proud of it, but always look carefully at the amount of variance the model explains. If the authors don't mention this, you can calculate it by moving the decimal place in the $r^2$ or adjusted $r^2$. So, if the $r^2$ is .25, it means that 25 per cent of the variance in the target variable is explained by the predictors in the model. A perfect model would give you a value of 1, which is 100 per cent prediction. However, models explaining small amounts of variance can be statistically significant. I've seen them as low as, for example, 15 per cent.

Let's think about that for a moment. A group of researchers have collected a range of data on a set of variables that they believe will explain a behaviour. In the end, they can explain 15 per cent of that behaviour. At least, that's roughly what it means. So, you can quite legitimately ask where the other 85 per cent went. Explaining such a small amount of variance in a set of scores, leaving the rest a complete mystery, is a lot less impressive than when the authors report the fact that this model is statistically significant. Use your critical thinking skills, spot this when you see it happening, and you can spend time discussing what might have gone wrong. You might like to think of additional variables that the researchers didn't test which might have improved the prediction. You'll get additional marks if you do this. Of course, you have to suggest sensible variables, not just anything.

## Borderline findings and margins of error

Imagine that you have just read a study that reports a survey in which 52 per cent of people think that the government is 'doing a good job'. In politics slight majorities can mean a great deal, and many governments stand and fall on tiny majorities. However, whenever you see statistics like these, ask yourself what the likely margin of error might be. There's always some error attached to any figures. That's why some researchers refer to confidence intervals. Therefore, we might say that we have a 95 per cent confidence interval around the proportions 48 and 56. That is, we are 95 per cent certain that the true figure rests between 48 and 56. That doesn't mean that 52 is correct, of course, just because it falls exactly between 48 and 56. In fact, we have a clear margin of error: remember that the 95 per cent certainty doesn't refer to the 52 itself, but to the true figure falling between 48 and 56.

## Clinical significance versus statistical significance

A related issue is that of clinical versus statistical significance. Just because an effect is statistically significant doesn't mean that it automatically is meaningful or applicable in day-to-day life, or even *detectable* in normal life! Effects that make a difference to people are what we call *clinically* significant.

Imagine that you read about some research into a treatment for Tourette's Syndrome which can reduce inappropriate swearing by an average of one episode per day in those people for whom swearing is a problem (since it does not affect all people with Tourette's). If it did that consistently across all participants, the effect could turn out to be statistically significant. However, you need to look at the size of the effect quite carefully. If you discover that the average person with Tourette's swears three times a day, then a reduction of one episode of the use of bad language is effectively a third. That is really worth doing. However, what if the average was *twenty*? Does an intervention that takes 20 episodes of swearing down to 19 really seem that impressive? It could be significant in a statistical sense, but clinically it would be almost valueless. Always look at the context of the claims made, and consider clinical significance alongside statistical significance. Do this even when the studies you are reading about aren't clinical: even cognitive psychology or social psychology can be analysed critically using the same principles. Are the reported effects big enough to mean anything in the real world?

Let us take another example. Imagine that a study in social psychology was reported in which the authors found that by altering the wording of an advertisement, sales of the product increased. Let's assume it is for potato crisps. Instead of the byline 'Crunch Yourself to Happiness', the crisp manufacturers tried 'Crunch Yourself Higher'. Of course, the company would welcome increased sales, naturally. However, what constitutes a meaningful increase in sales? An additional 500 boxes per month, month after month after month, might seem good: if you tried to eat 500 boxes of potato crisps per month you'd soon know just how much that is. However, what if sales were normally 250,000 boxes per month? The extra 500 is a drop in the ocean, and the company just wouldn't care; changing their advertising would cost them more than the increased revenue from sales, thus rendering it detrimental to the company.

Occasionally the reverse is true. Small effects are commonly non-significant statistically, but the mean difference in the analysis points to an effect that might still be useful for the individuals concerned. If you consider our example of Tourette's Syndrome, and you have evidence that suggests that people will take any reduction in their swearing behaviour, no matter how small, because it gives them hope of further advances and helps them achieve even more in the longer term, then it is worth it, even if the effect isn't impressive statistically. However, always remember that if the effect isn't significant, there's a very high chance that it might not really exist at all, and could be attributable to a chance fluctuation in the data. You'd need a replication to convince people that there's something small but robust happening.

There is a danger in going beyond non-significant results, especially trying to comment on a so-called 'non-significant trend'. A non-significant trend is, to most statisticians, equivalent to nothing. Whenever you see research papers referring to a 'trend that did not reach significance', imagine the same sentence with 'effect that does not exist'.

## Crime statistics

If ever there was a can of worms waiting to be opened, this is it. Crime statistics are used regularly by a range of agencies and academics, not just by psychologists. Or, perhaps, we ought to say they are *misused* regularly. In fact, it is worse than that. The figures themselves are inaccurate and problematic a lot of the time, and the interpretations and uses to which they are put are also misguided.

There is more than one source of crime statistics in the United Kingdom. One is the police figures, which of course only deal with *reported* crime; another is the British Crime survey, which deals only with what victims of crime report. Another could be insurance claim statistics. Can you see problems already?

Some people report crimes that haven't actually happened, especially when they are trying to defraud insurance companies and make claims. Other people don't report crimes to insurance companies because their policy excesses are larger than the losses. If you have a policy excess (the amount you agree to contribute yourself if something goes wrong) of £100, and someone has stolen £80 of items from you, it isn't worth reporting it to your insurers, even though you are legally contracted to do so, because the crime that occurred will affect your insurance premium for the future. The crime therefore won't show up in the insurers' statistics.

Police figures only feature crimes that *have* been reported. Therefore, there is bound to be additional crime that we know nothing about. This is often called the 'dark figure' of crime. Our biggest fear is often that this is much, much larger than reported crime, and the world is a much more terrifying place than we currently believe. The British Crime Survey (BCS) is likely to fill the gap in the police statistics, because it doesn't rely on reported crime. If you are one of the people surveyed in the BCS, you might report crimes that the police were never told about.

So a single source of crime statistics isn't necessarily useful: you should always question statistics from a single source. In addition, you should also question the statistics themselves. Never accept comparative statistics at face value, for example the numbers of cases of theft, rape or car crime in different countries. The definitions of those crimes can vary from country to country, and the social attitudes to each crime can also differ. Add to that variations in the individual country's criminal justice system (judges' attitudes, media pressure on the Courts and so on), and it makes comparisons extremely shaky.

Another problem concerns the stability of the statistics over time. As we know, a proportion of verdicts are fought in the Courts, and convictions are overturned sometimes. However, it can take so long for these cases to be heard that what was reported as a crime in 2002 could be overturned in 2006, but with no retrospective changes to the crime statistics for 2002. Be aware that a proportion of the crimes in the current statistics are not crimes at all, and will be void, although you would have to do a great deal of detective work to amend the figures and get a 'truer' picture.

Another problem with crime figures is that they need to be understood in terms of the whole population. Often we see numbers of crimes going up or down, but we need to know what the size of the population is in relation to it. We also need to think about the number of perpetrators. Sometimes, one person can be responsible for a peak in the figures for a particular time period, especially if they are very prolific offenders who evade capture for some time, or who commit a very large number of more unusual crimes in a very short space of time.

In Britain, the definition of violent crime has changed in the last decade or so, from something that the police define as violent to something that is defined by the experience of the victim. This means that violent crime figures are simply not comparable between prior to this change of definition and the present day.

There are hundreds, if not thousands, of major and minor changes to the reporting methods that create a minefield of hazards when interpreting the data. For psychologists interested in crime and others, we don't have our own crime statistics: we have to work with those that exist. This presents a severe restriction on the value of the work that we can do.

We can now turn to the application of critical thinking to some specific areas of psychology. It isn't feasible to look at every area of psychology, because this book would be fifty times larger if we tried. However, the sections that follow give you a flavour of the ways in which you can apply critical thinking in psychological fields. The principles apply across all of psychology and beyond.

# CRITICAL THINKING IN HEALTH PSYCHOLOGY

When it comes to health psychology, most of what we do involves critical thinking, and often at multiple levels. Health psychology typically involves the study of risk perception, for example. All of our understanding of probability comes into play, but in addition to that we need to grasp the issues surrounding subjective probability – that is, the study of what people *think* about chance and statistics, not the actual physical truth. Similarly, this invokes all of our knowledge about the gambler's fallacy, and also the nature of unrealistic optimism. Most negative health behaviours are predicated upon some kind of view that 'it won't happen to me'. Of course, this isn't something people can legitimately say, even though they think that they can. Oddly enough, it seems to work in a kind of nonsensical conjunction with the *availability heuristic*.

The availability heuristic, a term coined by Tversky and Kahneman (1974), is a description of the phenomenon whereby individuals judge the likelihood of something occurring by the ease with which they can imagine an example of it. People therefore think that things they have heard about a lot are more common than things they haven't heard about. To some extent this makes sense, but it starts to break down rather quickly the more you look at it. We hear a lot in the newspapers about violent crime, which often leads people to think that it is common. It isn't – it is generally much rarer than people imagine. The media, being obsessed with scandal and sensationalism, overplay such stories and repeat them. It's a form of reporting bias. This means that every time something bad happens, you get told about it. When most good things happen, you hear nothing. Furthermore, every time nothing happens, it's just silence all round. However, this doesn't quite explain health choices, because people use the availability heuristic differently then. They don't just seem to make risk assessments based on the availability of examples: they appear to decide what they prefer to believe, and then make risk assessments based on the availability of examples that provide evidence for that belief!

For example, smoking, as we know, leads to all sorts of diseases. Most people will probably be able to think of people they have known who are either suffering from smoking-related diseases like emphysema or who have lost their lives to lung cancer or a similar condition. However, a smoker might wish to believe that the chances of succumbing to a smoking-related illness are small. Therefore, they ignore the cases that don't support this, and instead a smaller number of cases that don't prove the point can become prominent. For instance, we have all heard of smokers who refer you to their grandparent who smoked nine million cigarettes a day since the age of four and lived to be 150. I'm exaggerating, of course, but it's a common story. Unrealistic optimism appears to stem from a perverse use of the availability heuristic. Making that kind of point in a health psychology essay will win you a few marks, and is a perfect example of thinking critically. Add some discussion of the phenomenon above with a knowledge of the *confirmation bias*, as this effect is known, and you can really start to figure out what is going on. Confirmation bias is the tendency to accept data that confirm what you already believe. Can you see how it is all starting to fit together?

Redelmeier and Tversky (1996) report that traditionally people believe that arthritis pain is worse in cold or wet weather. Despite a lack of any evidence, both the public and many doctors have this belief. A small-scale study over a year showed no relationship between arthritis pain and the weather (as indexed by air pressure) in the sample. However, when a group of students were shown the graphs of the statistically non-significant correlations between these factors, they genuinely reported 'seeing' a relationship in the figures, despite the complete lack of it. The authors concluded that 'beliefs about arthritis pain and the weather may tell more about the workings of the mind than of the body' (p.2896).

## Complementary and alternative medicine

The entire field of complementary and alternative medicine (CAM) is of great interest to those of us involved in healthcare, and it is a growing area of research amongst health psychologists, myself included. To me, it is an excellent example of a world where critical thinking is essential. As a health psychologist with an interest in critical thinking, CAM allows me to put both to good use. The CAM field is packed with examples of debates and arguments that may or may not adhere well to principles of logic.

Firstly, it is important to state that not all CAM approaches are the same, and there is an important distinction between complementary and alternative approaches which certain practitioners don't always make. Alternative approaches are something sold to us to use *instead* of orthodox modern medicine. This in itself could represent a danger. Complementary approaches, in contrast, are intended to be used *alongside* orthodox medicine. However, in terms of measurement of efficacy, these distinctions don't necessarily matter that much. The key debate centres on whether CAM works or not. For many, CAM approaches are little more than placebos, but for some they mean a lot more. As psychologists we really ought to be interested in placebo effects, even if that's all there is to a particular remedy. We can take a very structured approach to studying CAM in relation to its effects and effectiveness, which overlaps somewhat with the approaches that medical scientists would choose to take.

Firstly, there is the issue of whether they work. To some researchers, the gold standard for testing a CAM is the same as the gold standard for testing anything, which is the experimental approach, in particular the randomised controlled trial (RCT; Van Wersch, Forshaw, & Cartwright, 2009). Immediately, however, we run into problems. It seems straight-forward to most scientists to say that one should test an intervention by applying it to a group of people; give another group a false version without telling them; doing nothing at all with a third group; then compare them. Thus we have a treatment group, a placebo group and a do-nothing control. We need to know not only if *believing* whether something works means that it works, but also whether people sometimes get better when you don't give them any treatment whatever. (Note that this is only ethical when we have no evidence that the treatment works.) Spontaneous recovery does occur, and we need to take it into account. A true placebo effect is what you get when you take the do-nothing scores away from the placebo group scores: what is left is the placebo effect. You compare this with the effects, if observed, of the real treatment.

Without spending thousands of pages telling you all about the evidence for and against the many hundreds of CAM approaches that exist, not all CAM boils down to placebo, but at the present time the evidence for CAM isn't particularly strong, and the evidence against is more overwhelming. To sum it up, the split is something in the region of 90/10. That is, about 90 per cent of CAM appears to do nothing, or virtually nothing, and about 10 per cent seem to have some effect, some of the time, in some people. It is crucial to compare this with the effectiveness of orthodox treatments. Not all things done by doctors work all of the time, and even when they do work they are not perfect cures. The split is better than 90/10, but it certainly isn't 100/0.

The arguments that some people who are in favour of CAM use to explain away the research evidence – or lack of it – substantiating these practices are interesting. They commonly claim that the RCT isn't the right way to research CAM. That begs the question of what the right way is. When they do explain what that might be, it is often some kind of nebulous interview approach which asks people who use CAM if it worked for them. This rides roughshod over psychologists' knowledge of effects such as reporting bias, the sharpshooter fallacy and so on – we simply cannot rely on the evidence of our senses to tell us if something has 'worked'. We also cannot rely on memory or a lack of comparison. What is most interesting is that on the relatively rare occasions when the RCT research *does* show an effect that can be attributed to CAM, the CAM supporters do not reject it. If the RCT is the wrong method, then surely it should be ignored, no matter what the results?

Quantum mechanical explanations are of particular interest in relation to CAM, and are often referred to by CAM supporters, albeit in a rather unusual way. CAM regularly resorts to explanations about 'forces' and 'energies', and these are rarely presented to us in terms that match today's scientific theories. That in itself can be a problem, but a much bigger one is the inconsistent use of quantum theories to support CAM. The quantum world is a strange, counterintuitive one, which also takes into account the observer and the method of observation, which means that quantum explanations incorporate a sense of subjectivity. However, that doesn't mean that the quantum world is a licence to believe *anything*. The electron can be conceived as a particle or as a wave. Furthermore, it can be measured as a particle or a wave, depending on what you choose to expect it to be, determined by how you measure it. That might seem mysterious, but it's true. However, this gives us a clear message: looking for something makes it happen. This is the exact opposite of what CAM supporters often say when we fail to find an effect in trials of CAM. Commonly, they argue that the effects of CAM are somehow *pushed away* when we subject them to analysis and scrutiny. They argue that the vital energy forces are interfered with when we study them. Surely if one is trying to apply quantum observations like wave–particle duality to much larger-scale effects like treatments for disease, then the principles cannot reverse themselves? The effects possibly might reflect what one looks for, not the very opposite.

Another problem is that the 'energy fields' that many CAM approaches rely on are rarely defined. Modern orthodox medicine isn't just about doing things that seem to work: we look for reasons, connections and mechanisms for things based upon the massive body of knowledge that has arisen over centuries of study. Instead, CAM supporters often simply refer to 'forces'. It's not uncommon for them to stop there. They also refer to 'tradition' to back up what they suggest to us. Apparently, if something has been happening for centuries, it must have substance. This makes no sense at all. Whilst persistence through time is a characteristic of 'facts' about intensely tested phenomena in traditional science, it isn't the same for untested theories.

Two things persist through time. The first type is 'real' phenomena. They persist because they make sense, and are hard to deny, despite attempts to do so. The second concerns unfalsifiable ideas that refer to untestable notions like 'vital forces'. Because no one can ever disprove the idea that a magic carrot makes us believe that the earth is rotating when it isn't, that idea can persist forever if people tell each other about it. That doesn't mean that the magic carrot theory of planetary rotation is just as acceptable as the idea that we have an immune system that helps us to fight both endogenous and exogenous threats to our health. Everything we learn about the body is consistent with the existence of the immune system. The idea persists because it makes sense, over and over again, and slots nicely in with everything else we know. The magic carrot isn't part of anything. It just sits there in our heads. 'Untestable' and 'unfalsifiable' *does not* mean 'true'. A failure to recognise this is the fundamental flaw in reasoning that helps some rather unusual ideas to flourish.

Other common dismissals of the lack of evidence supporting CAM, even when scientists have tried to find that evidence, include unnecessary personal attacks on the scientists and claims that they are biased and prejudiced, and counter-evidence in the form of testimonials from 'satisfied customers'. Have a look on the websites of CAM practitioners, and you will often find statements from people (whose existence we can't verify) saying things like 'I was feeling dreadful and the doctor didn't know what was wrong with me, but I tried X therapy and in days I felt right as rain again', or 'My eczema cleared up after just two sessions of X therapy'. Unfortunately, many CAM practitioners have no training in scientific research methods and simply fail to grasp, perhaps, that this does not constitute proper evidence.

Let us answer some of these common misconceptions.

**Time after time I have treated patients successfully** What figures do you have to support this? What is your benchmark for having 'treated' someone? What constitutes success? How many people do you see that never come back to you and never communicate with you again? We need to assume that every one of those did not see any benefit from your approach. What is the proportion of happy customers to people who never returned and never give feedback?

**A positive outcome in CAM isn't the same as a positive outcome in a drug trial**  Isn't this just like saying that drugs have to work, whereas CAM doesn't? But if CAM doesn't work, what is it for?

**CAM treats the whole person, not just a symptom**  This is a perfectly acceptable statement to make of itself. That would make a CAM much better than conventional medicine. That's excellent. Now I need to know what measures are being used to demonstrate these holistic benefits. Are the benefits both physical and psychological? Which health outcomes are under test, and where is the evidence that the effects exist and persist over an appreciable length of time?

**CAM treatments are not all the same**  Don't mix up therapies which complement orthodox medicine with those that could be dangerous because they lay claim to cures by themselves. We accept that complementary approaches don't compete with orthodox medicine – they complement it. That is acceptable, superficially. However, complementing something does not mean that there is no requirement to demonstrate effectiveness. If I tell you that taking a painkiller is important, but that my yellow hats, at a cost of £10 each, will complement the effect of the painkiller, I should be able to *show* that my yellow hats do actually increase the effect of the painkiller in some way. I can't just *say* it.

**CAM approaches are not harmful, so they do not need to be 'tested' or 'prove' themselves**  Firstly, this presupposes that CAM approaches are not harmful. Without any testing, how can we know that? Secondly, most CAM practitioners do not sell their therapies on the grounds that they don't do any harm – their claims are that they do some *good*. Again, there is a burden of proof here. Or at least that's how orthodox medical scientists see it.

# CRITICAL THINKING IN COGNITIVE PSYCHOLOGY

Cognitive psychology is an area that lends itself very well to demonstrating that you have critical thinking skills. It's a massive field, so we can only skim the surface here, but there are always things to say about studies in cognitive psychology, because most of them involve some key issues.

One critical view of many studies is that you can't actually control what people think. Not only that, neither can they. If you are comparing, for example, two mnemonic strategies, you have to instruct your participants to use them and hope that they do. So not only do you have the problem that the participants might not have done what you asked, even if they tried to, but you have an even bigger problem, which is that they might have done other things too. Whether volitionally or not, they could have adapted or changed the strategies you gave them, or added other techniques. To some extent this problem is spread across all conditions of your experiment, so it shouldn't systematically cling to one condition. However, what if one of your conditions causes people to reflect on their memory processes in a way that the others don't, and they end up doing extra things in that condition over and above random interference? Your study comparing X, Y and Z then becomes a comparison of X, Y and Z with a bit of X and some P and a J.

What if your memory study involves lists of words or objects? Where do you get those lists from? Most published studies report painstaking work to prepare word lists for use in such studies, but rarely are they without problems. Always pay close attention to stimulus lists in published cognitive studies. You might find some interesting anomalies. If the authors claim that the words were 'unrelated', look for connections you can make quite easily between the words that might prove them wrong. If they claim the words all consist of two syllables, look for words that in certain accents are three syllables long, and so on. For example, in the UK, the word 'totally' is three syllables long in RP (received pronunciation). However, in different accents, it is not. Without using international phonetic symbols is it very difficult to show how these words sound in various accents, and most psychologists are unfortunately not familiar with those symbols unless they study psycholinguistics. In the North East of England, for example, most people would say 'totally' as if it had two syllables, 'to'lly'. There are lots of other examples. 'Sovereign' can be pronounced by some with two syllables, by others with three. Furthermore, in RP English the word 'poor' has a single syllable. In other accents, including some from the North West of England, it has two, as if it were 'poo-er'.

The situation becomes more complex when overseas English speakers are considered. In most accents of American English, the word 'new' rhymes with 'too', and 'sue' and is pronounced as if it were spelled 'soo'. In RP British English the 'n' is nasalised, making it sound more like 'nyoo'. Similarly, in US English there is little or no difference between the way a person says 'rider' and the way they say 'writer', whereas in many other parts of the world you can clearly hear that they are different. If a study uses rhyming or other aspects of phonetic structure as part of its stimulus development, look carefully at issues that could mean that the work doesn't travel well across the Atlantic, or only works for a proportion of the population.

Sometimes word lists claim to be of abstract nouns only, which might be crucial to the running of a study. Abstract nouns are those referring to an idea that cannot be seen or touched. The best example is possibly 'love'. Such nouns are contrasted with *concrete* nouns, which are things you can directly experience with the senses, like 'fruit', 'car', 'crab' or 'moon'. Imagine you saw this list of abstract nouns in a stimulus list used by experimental psychologists:

*Notion, harm, ethic, lie, pride, comfort, grace, skill, beauty, aspiration*

Can you see any problems? From left to right, 'notion' seems fine. I can't touch a notion, smell one or taste one, and I don't know what a notion looks like. However, I know what it is. 'Harm' is pretty much the same, as is 'ethic'. What about 'lie'? Again, you can't smell, taste or touch a lie. 'Pride' is an interesting word, which commonly features on lists of abstract nouns. The trouble is, pride is a *polysemous lexeme*, which is the fancy linguistic term for a word with two different meanings or uses. One of the two is abstract, but the other is not. When we say 'pride comes before a fall', 'pride' is an abstract noun. However, what about 'a pride of lions'? If you happen to think of that meaning instead of the other one, you immediately have a mental picture. You *can* see, feel, smell and hear a pride, not that I'd recommend trying to touch one. What about 'comfort'? That is fine, but 'grace'?

Grace is interesting, because as a common noun it is abstract, but because it is also a proper noun, the name for a woman, many people can conjure up a mental image of someone called Grace. If they do, it ceases to be abstract in their mental list. 'Skill' is ok, although you'd be hard-pressed to imagine skill without getting a mental image of a carpenter, a footballer, an artist or someone like that. You might unintentionally concretise the abstraction. 'Beauty' is difficult too, because for most people the instant thought is of physical, visual beauty, so a picture emerges without conscious effort. Finally, 'aspiration' seems acceptable. For most of us, this word doesn't summon up any specific images. However, to a linguist it refers to the process of emitting a blast of air on pronouncing certain sounds, like the 'p' in the word 'posy'. So, for them, aspiration can be felt and heard, so it has a concrete version.

I think I have made enough of a point about this now. Not only should you construct your own stimuli very carefully, and seek lots of advice from different people, you should also look very closely at others' stimuli. Scrutinise every word for issues that the authors haven't spotted, then try to create an argument for why what you have spotted might influence the results. This is the most important point. If what you noticed is unlikely to make any difference, then pointing it out is not going to get you better marks. However, if it is, you're onto something, and your marks will shoot up.

# CRITICAL THINKING IN SOCIAL PSYCHOLOGY

Social psychology is so rich in pickings for critical thinking that there is even a branch of it, critical social psychology, which is like a festival of critical thinking applied to social and societal situations, as part of which all scenes and situations are regarded as more or less social and socially constructed. The first place to start being critical about social psychology is in relation to the methods used, which opens up the bigger debate of psychological methods in general.

Social psychologists often use experimental methods, and equally often they rely on observation. This is usually dictated by the nature of the thing they are trying to study. You can't experiment on behaviour that occurs naturally, because that interferes with it. In these cases, you have to simply let it happen and watch it. Theories are then built around those observations. As you will know, observational studies can be picked apart because we have to make inferences from what we see, which reduces our ability to determine cause and effect. For example, if we observe that more coffee is being sold at a time when there are more incidences of aggressive behaviour in a café, we could assume that drinking coffee increases aggression, but it might actually be that aggressive people drink more coffee. This, overall, reduces the value of our findings.

Experimental social psychology gets around these problems by directly manipulating the variables in question, but immediately runs the risk of being seen as something artificial, or ecologically invalid. Always look carefully at the tasks people have been asked to perform in experimental social research. Do they extend out into real-life situations easily? For example, if people are asked to estimate the credibility of an expert speaker in an experimental situation, is that the same as the judgement they would make of an expert in the real world, perhaps backed by the media and word-of-mouth? Social psychologists cannot manipulate the real world to conduct studies: instead they try to emulate it in small-scale studies. Do they succeed in creating the conditions that emulate the outside world?

The next area of criticism relates to the social psychology of attitudes. Most attitude studies involve surveys, and require respondents to agree or disagree to some extent using a Likert scale. Far too often students take these scales for granted. However, the next time you are trying to generate a critique of a study that has used some kind of measurement instrument like this, look at the instrument itself. Do not take it for granted that it made sense to the participants, or that every statement in the instrument means one thing and only one thing. Look for potential sources of confusion, ambiguity, or examples where the language used reduces the applicability of the instrument and therefore the results. Would the instrument 'work' in the UK if it was designed for an American audience, and vice versa?

Social psychology is a fascinating area, and its findings are relevant for other parts of psychology almost without exception. Look for ways in which you can see those connections. Social psychologists have pointed out the many ways in which people exhibit bias and prejudice, towards themselves, towards others and towards facts, figures and the things that they perceive. This applies to the scientists conducting the research in addition to the participants in that research. Look for ways in which the lessons of social psychology are applicable everywhere, including outside and within social psychology. This is a particularly important point, because there is a crucial problem with social constructionist arguments that is like the proverbial 'elephant in the room': everyone can see it, but no one dares mention it. But if everything is socially constructed, then so is the entire notion that everything is socially constructed. Social psychologists don't really have an answer to this, except to point out that they accept it but somehow embrace the idea, rather than trying to *pretend* that they can be value-free, objective and neutral. That's perfectly ok – except that everything they say, including this, is a social construct. It goes on and on and on.

One particular criticism of social psychology which you should avoid making is that its findings are somehow 'common sense'. Firstly, common sense doesn't exist, because that would mean that the whole human race would think something, and there is virtually nothing that the whole human race thinks collectively. Secondly, social psychology has a wealth of evidence backing up its ideas, while common sense hasn't got a single piece of research behind it. Thirdly, common sense contradicts itself. 'Many hands make light work', but we are told that 'too many cooks spoil the broth'. Equally, we should cross our bridges when we come to them, but never put off until tomorrow what we can do today. When a social psychologist finds something out about how people act under the influence of other people, they might confirm something you had thought, but that doesn't make the study worthless, or common sense.

In a social psychology study that makes the point about such sayings rather beautifully, Teigen (1986) presented students with statements in two forms, one a reversal of the other, and noted that sometimes both seemed to be judged as true. For example, an original proverb is 'Wise men make proverbs and fools repeat them'. This was reversed to say 'Fools make proverbs and wise men repeat them'. Students rated both as true; common sense is to be found where, exactly?

# CRITICAL THINKING IN BIOLOGICAL PSYCHOLOGY

Biological psychology is an area to which you really need to apply critical thinking. It is easy to be 'blinded with science' by biological psychologists, because they use so many complicated terms that you can get quite lost; there is a tendency to think that everything sounds rather clever, and so it is difficult to see holes in arguments. However, very often biological psychologists concentrate entirely on generating explanations of behaviour that don't take the wider social context into account. They assume, very often, that all brains work the same way, when in fact they often don't. Always stop and ask yourself if the answers they are providing really do explain everything.

Sometimes Occam's Razor isn't the answer. It is a very sensible way to proceed, by assuming that the simplest explanation that fits the facts is the best one. However, in human life, most behaviours are multivariate, so any single explanation is unlikely to fit the facts particularly well. People are complicated, and are affected by potentially dozens if not hundreds of factors. It is usually too simple to suggest that people's biological makeup explains their behaviour, except in the most simple of situations, usually in relation to perceptual phenomena such as how a sound is heard or a ray of light is detected.

Most biological psychologists are careful not to lay claim to a perfect explanation of human antics, but watch out for cases where they go beyond the data. A common issue is that of causality. Links between biochemical processes in the brain and signs and symptoms do not necessarily show us *how* the two are linked. Indeed, some criticise biological psychologists for being overly descriptive, rather than explaining *how* things work. A classic causality problem, for example, is that we see various biochemical aberrations in the brains of people who are depressed. We are still not sure whether being depressed creates the biochemical imbalances, or whether the chemical problem starts first and the depression follows. Even if we did know that the chemical imbalance came first, we are still some way from knowing why that would happen. Only when we can predict who will develop the imbalance can we prevent depression occurring.

Psychology is an infant science. Just because we don't have all the answers yet isn't a reason for giving up and not trying to make advances and discoveries. Biological psychologists are no different from any other type, and we all have these issues to work around.

## CHAPTER 4 – CRITICAL QUESTIONS

1. What does a critical analysis about psychology tell us about psychology itself?
2. 'When you analyse psychology critically, there's just nothing left worth doing.' Discuss.

# 5  Putting Critical Thinking to Use: Getting Good Grades

Have you ever wondered what other students do to get higher or lower grades than you? Sometimes it's just as fascinating to ponder lower scores as higher scores. We all want higher grades, one assumes, but we often don't think about analysing what leads to a lower grade than our own, because we think we don't need to. However, that's like saying that you never need to look backwards as well as forwards. If some people score higher than you, you need to know what they are doing that you aren't. However, the same logic applies to those people who score lower than you. If a low mark means a student has lots of things wrong and few things right, and a high mark means lots of things right and very little wrong, then someone in the middle must be doing a balanced mixture of wrong things and right things. Most of you reading this will be somewhere in the middle – that's just a matter of logic and statistics.

## Sample mini-essays: compare and contrast

Compare the following mini-essays. They are presented in order of increasing excellence, from one that failed to one that achieved a first-class mark. I have deliberately avoided lots of references and citations, because they will just get in the way of what I am trying to demonstrate: instead, we are interested in the quality of the arguments made and, of course, their relevance. Quality plus relevance equals marks. It's a simple equation that few students really grasp at first.

So we will forget about references to studies for these examples: that's a simple part that can be added, as citations increase the mark when they are relevant. This essay is about ideas. You can try taking the best one and adding your own references and citations, to see how much it will improve. Often, essays that get better marks are better written, use good grammar and so on. I have produced these examples without that complication: the grammar quality is consistent across the essays, although the sophistication of the vocabulary isn't. Finally, word count also helps to determine a mark. Writing too much or too little is seen as evidence of 'poor scholarship'. In each example, I have used precisely 500 words, as the question requires, to make comparison simpler. In the real world, real essays differ in many ways, which makes the job of marking work quite difficult at times.

> Critically evaluate, in no more than 500 words, the contribution of psychology to the understanding of intelligence.

## Failed essay

Psychology is the scientific study of the mind and everything that a person does. Ever since people first started using tools and thinking, they have valued intelligence and pondered over what makes one person 'clever' and another person not. Psychologists do not always study intelligence, for example some work in other areas, but some of the early psychologists were extremely interested in intellect.

Psychologists try to measure the things that they encounter in the world, and intelligence is no different. If we can decide what intelligence is and measure it, then we can do useful things with the concept, and even make people more intelligent, in theory.

The main problem is that different psychologists have different ideas about what makes up intelligence, so they cannot agree, which means that they cannot work together. What one person calls intelligence another one would not, and in different cultures intelligence is thought of differently. Most of the work that psychologists have done has concentrated on ideas of intelligence that are concerned with problem solving and the use of the mind rather than physical skills like making a cabinet or fixing a problem with a burst water pipe. It might be that for some people in some societies it is more valuable to work with the hands rather than do all sorts of complicated mathematical and philosophical things that are not of any use to the world.

Many of the psychologists got around the problem of defining intelligence by saying that it is what intelligence tests measure, but in my opinion that just avoids the issue. Intelligence tests should be devised that test whatever the people in a society judge is intelligence. Therefore, psychologists should start by interviewing people about what they think intelligence is before they create their tests. That way the tests would be more ecologically valid and this would prevent some of the political problems that measuring intelligence creates.

Some psychologists have used intelligence tests to help employers decide who the best person for a job is, or even to deny people their rights. Another use of the intelligence test is to find out if a child in school needs extra help to achieve their goals and learn properly. Therefore there can be both good and bad uses of intelligence tests and so we should not decide that studying intelligence is always a bad thing. For example, if we know why someone is not performing well we can help them, especially if we know which bit of their intelligence, such as their memory or their use of language, is giving them problems. Something wrong with memory can make a person seem less intelligent than they really are.

In conclusion, intelligence means many things to many people, and any one definition is not going to provide all of the answers we need. Psychologists have studied intelligence in their own ways, but different people from various countries and cultures have their own views that might be different, and these should not be ignored.

## Moderate essay

Psychologyhasbeenattheforefrontofourscientificexplorationsof intelligence, because intelligence is a psychological phenomenon.

Every person has some kind of individual version of what intelligence is, from mental skill, through to problem solving ability or even genius. Most of us would claim that we can spot an intelligent person or a person of limited intelligence without too much difficulty. In this essay we will identify the contribution made by psychology to our understanding of intelligence.

From the early days of psychology, at the start of the twentieth century, psychologists have taken an interest in intelligence, particularly in order to create tests to tell the difference between children who showed promise or potential and those who perhaps did not. Today we would see this as somewhat unacceptable, which in some ways shows that we have developed in our attitudes.

We still have not come to any firm conclusion about what intelligence is, and the work of various psychologists has clarified in some ways but has confused in others. The common-sense notion of intelligence has been debated and examined time and time again, but we do not yet have any model of intelligence that is particularly more useful than that common-sense one. Some psychologists say that there is only one thing called intelligence, but others argue that it has many specific components and sub-components, which implies that a person can be intelligent in one domain and not in others. The line between intelligence and skill is a fine one, and the concept of expertise cuts across that line. Is an expert always intelligent? To some, this would depend on the nature of the expertise, although some case studies of autistic-type experts (i.e. savants) suggest that it is possible to have an isolated area of expertise in an otherwise normal or less-intelligent person.

Intelligence testing has been shown to be flawed, for example where some children could not answer the questions, not because they were unintelligent, but because the items presented to them did not fit within their cultural framework. For instance, odd-one-out tasks might not work in cultures where the concept of finding the odd one out is unheard of. There is quite a big difference between not being able to complete a task and not understanding the instructions for a task. Sometimes a simple thing can sound complicated when you attempt to describe it, especially to someone who isn't familiar with it.

However, without intelligence testing and research into human abilities, we might not be able to discover if the right person is being hired for a job, or whether a child has a developmental delay that can be treated. There are some important advantages to taking the study of intelligence seriously, which lead to advances for humankind.

In this essay we have considered the potential positive and negative contributions that psychologists have made to our understanding of intelligence. We might have come a long way, but there is still most of the way to go.

## Excellent essay

Intelligence is a nebulous concept that psychologists have always struggled to define. One could argue that, as our methods of investigation have become more sophisticated, so our contentment with glib definitions of abstract ideas has drastically reduced. Learning more makes us realise how little we really do know.

Early psychologists concerned themselves with testing intelligence, primarily for use in educational contexts, and even that endeavour wasn't without its political dimension. Put simply, the moment we begin to set people apart on the basis of their skills or faculties, we open ourselves up to criticism, even when our intentions are good, and even abuse of our findings can follow.

Different theories of intelligence vary in the relative contributions of crystallised or fluid elements (what you have learned versus what you can do with it), or the numbers of factors that make up our overall 'brightness' or 'intellect'. Some say intelligence is two things, some dozens. To some extent, this argument mirrors the nature of the debate between monotheistic and pantheistic religions, which conceptualise their deity as either one or more distinct entities. At heart, the theories and values are often similar, regardless of the number of gods.

Fundamentally, however, most people do seem to agree that Einstein had greater intellectual capacity than Homer Simpson (deliberately avoiding the insensitivity of choosing a living being as an example of a person of lower intelligence) and that this means something for what they are likely to achieve and to contribute to the sum of the world's knowledge. What psychologists studying intelligence have done is to try to capture this common understanding and derive shared principles from it.

It is far too easy to argue that psychologists have done more harm than good in studying intelligence. True, we have made errors along the path to wherever it is we are going, but we have learned from our mistakes too. We now understand, painfully, that Western, white, middle-class conceptions of what it means to be bright have poisoned and biased our attempts to derive a universal view of what intellect is. However, on the positive side, we now know much more about how to support and encourage the less bright to maximise their potential. Separating dyslexia and ADHD from the notion of lower intelligence has moved us forward significantly. One could argue that our devotion to fathoming intelligence has helped create a more civilised and humane society. Through our errors, we become better people, more tolerant people.

The crucial consideration in evaluating the contribution of psychologists to our understanding of intelligence lies in the Socratic question 'what for'? To what ends have we pursued this examination of a factor that divides person from person, child from child, and sometimes, ostensibly, nation from nation? We can no longer hide behind dispassionate science for its own sake. If studying intelligence leads us to ways of improving the human condition, then it is worth it. If it leads to discrimination and prejudice, then we must stop, right here.

Can you see the clear difference between the three pieces? We can dwell on what each essay achieves (or doesn't) for a moment.

The first of these suffers in a number of ways. The language is uninspiring and repetitive. The essay is also repetitive, and some of the paragraphs are very short. There is a lack of flow, and the writer is really only making one point, and in many places you can counter their argument very easily. For example, there's nothing wrong in defining intelligence in terms of mental skill, which means that physical skills do not count. That isn't the same as saying that people with strong physical talents are somehow inferior to people with strong mental skills. They are just different, but the writer of this rather weak essay seems to mix those up. Furthermore, there is nothing memorable about the conclusion, which simply repeats the main argument again, and no signs of rhetoric or sensitivity to language. Finally, the question asks for 'critical evaluation', but there is very little of it present. The author mainly churns out a couple of textbook criticisms of research and theory in the area of intelligence, but makes no new points.

The middle essay is, well, 'middling'. It isn't spectacular or entirely original, but it is on the subject, it doesn't drift too much, and the language used is fair and reasonable, if not particularly sophisticated. It falls between the two other essays. There is an argument, and nothing in the essay is irrelevant. Probably the most important thing about this essay is that you could use it as the starting point to write a much better one. You probably could not say that about the first essay, the one that failed. In terms of learning from this exercise, this is an important point: really poor essays don't give you much to work on in order to improve them – you would often be better off starting from scratch. However, mediocre essays, or what we might refer to as 'pedestrian' work, do give you something to work from. A lecturer can polish them up and show a student what could be improved quite easily.

This is analogous to any number of other real-world situations. If you bring me a barely shaped piece of clay, it isn't worth trying to decorate and glaze it and turn it into an item of pottery. Start again, and reshape the clay from scratch. If you fail a piece of work, my advice is to rethink your approach. The old approach didn't work, and trying to shine it up won't take you very far. In motoring terminology, you have to think about whether you have a repair or a write-off on your hands. This can be very depressing and demotivating. However, admitting to yourself that you've messed something up and taking control over the issue and tackling it can be liberating and empowering. We all make mistakes, and almost everyone has done something really stupid once or twice. Accept it when it happens and be positive.

Similarly, if you receive middling marks for a piece of work, be proud of what you have, and think carefully how you can make those marks higher, because it is within your grasp to do so. If you are one of those people who keeps on getting first-class marks, well done. Remember, however, that it's not all about the grades. Your education and development goes well beyond that, so you should always try to push yourself further and into new avenues.

The best of the essays is, to most people, probably markedly better than the other two. In places the language is possibly a little 'fancy', and sometimes students think that this is a bad thing. However, don't mistake fancy for pompous. If the language is correctly used, then it's fine. If you use fancy words incorrectly, then you do look silly. The last essay is flowing, and there are clear points being made in each paragraph, which implicitly helps the structure to emerge. The conclusion says something new, and ends with a strong rhetorical device, where an ending is referred to in the ending of the essay itself. There are some original points, such as the analogical reasoning between religious diversity and inconsistency of theory in intelligence research, and the writer avoids repetition, being able to select from a wide variety of terms from within their vocabulary. The essay is balanced, presenting arguments for and against the contributions of psychology to our understanding of intelligence, the writer stays close to the essay title, and, finally, you actually leave the essay with a clear picture of the opinion being presented, and you don't feel like that opinion is put forward without being explained or supported.

Hopefully this has been useful to you in seeing just what lecturers look for when determining whether an essay has been successful. It isn't mysterious or magic, but it isn't something we can explain in a single sentence, and we rarely have the time to write sample essays to show you what we're getting at. The law usually prevents us from showing you other people's essays. It is quite frustrating when you know that your essay was better than some but worse than others, but you aren't allowed to see what that means by comparison.

# UNDERSTANDING FEEDBACK

One of the biggest problems students report is that they don't understand feedback from lecturers on their work. One of the main problems lecturers cite is that of students not reading their feedback! It is common for students to take note of the mark given, and only the mark, ignoring what has been written both on a script and on a feedback sheet. What some students don't realise (although thankfully many do) is that the mark alone doesn't tell you very much at all. It tells you where on the ladder you are, but it doesn't tell you why. That's like waking up in the middle of a field with a slip of paper giving you your coordinates. You know exactly where you are, but that's not the most important thing to know right now. When you first wake, you will probably ask yourself 'Where am I?', but a split second later you'll want to know how you got there, and that is the question you'll be most preoccupied with.

So, the first lesson for any student is to read feedback and to understand the mark you have been given in the light of the commentary provided. But not every student always understands what has been written: it's as if the lecturer and the student speak different languages. The onus is on the student to learn that language, because it's a tried-and-tested way of communicating a lot of information succinctly, even if it is confusing at first.

It's not that hard to understand the language of feedback, but the problem is that very few universities provide students with a 'dictionary' to help them. Hopefully this section of the book will serve that purpose.

## Politeness

While not all feedback is polite, most of us try to convey our ideas without being rude or insulting, which often means that we choose phrases that play down errors and break them to you gently. However, if we skirt around an issue to protect your feelings, we obfuscate our feedback. Look out for phrases like 'Some good ideas but . . .' Another favourite is 'I can see that you have done a lot of research for this answer, however . . .' The crucial thing here is to make the most of the positive feedback, since your lecturer won't lie to you, but also to consider the negative. The biggest mistake a student can make is taking in only good comments and ignoring bad ones. As lecturers, we try to make it easier by being as polite about the bad as we can, but never to hide from it. Facing up to feedback is an important skill to learn.

Even when the news is bad, the whole point of feedback is to help you to produce better work in future. Don't fall into the mistake of thinking that because each piece of work you do is different, you can't learn from one in order to improve the next. The vast majority of feedback on student work is generic in nature, and we see students making the same mistakes over and over again, regardless of the essay question, unless they learn from their feedback.

## Being too descriptive

These days many lecturers wish that they had a rubber stamp that says 'Too descriptive and not enough critical insight'. It would save a lot of time. Over and over again students use up valuable words telling the reader about what other people have said, done and published. That helps to set the scene, but many essays don't require it. Look carefully at the question you have been set. Does it ask you to describe Theory X or Study Y? If it doesn't specifically demand this of you, then do not waste more than a sentence or two on them. Unless you are specifically told to describe something, the question setter really wants you to get on with analysing, debating and evaluating.

Let's use an analogy from outside psychology again. Most essays you will be set come in the form of *Critically evaluate the use of apples in modern cuisine*. This means that you have to get on with the task of explaining how and when apples are used, and weighing up the advantages and disadvantages of apples in various recipes. I'm sure you agree with that – so why would most students begin with a whole paragraph, or even a page, like this?

> The apple is a fleshy fruit of the genus Malus, available in thousands of varieties and commonly occurring in largely green or largely red types, although pink and yellow skins also are found. Modern apples are the result of thousands of years of cultivation, and constitute one of the world's largest fruit crops.

The question did not ask for a description of an apple. In reality, you'd probably get away with an introductory statement like this, but nothing more. Do not be tempted to continue like this.

In psychology the equivalent problem often involves issues such as explaining particular theories in detail instead of simply citing the original authors, or giving biographical details of famous researchers. For example, a common question might be *Critically evaluate the contribution of Piaget to modern developmental psychology*. Try to avoid writing a page like this:

> Piaget was born in the Swiss town of Neuchâtel in 1896, and spent the early part of his life being primarily interested in biology, and published on molluscs before beginning to develop a fascination with more psychological and psychoanalytical explanations of behaviour. He referred to his theories as belonging in the realm of genetic epistemology and often made use of his own three children to generate vast amounts of data.

And so it could go on – and often does, with students getting carried away. However, at no point did anyone ask who Piaget was or what kind of cheese he liked. That's all very interesting, but not called for in the question.

## Academic style

Have you ever received comments such as 'Content is good, but you must learn to write in a more suitable style'? If you have, what the writer is telling you is that you must write in a way that reflects the standards of writing in higher-end publications. If you have wondered what both achieves the best marks and impresses people, it's a combination of really relevant content, original ideas and good writing. There is an arbitrary quality to good writing, in that people have decided what is an appropriate way to phrase things and what isn't, but now that we have settled on an academic style of writing, we need to 'play the game'.

So what do you have to do to write more 'academically'? Let's begin with what it doesn't mean. Firstly, you don't have to write in very long sentences, and you don't have to use uncommon or long words all the time. The trick is to have a mixture of longer and shorter sentences and common and less common words. If you always write using short sentences, your work gets tedious and feels like a children's book. Similarly, you shouldn't just use simple words, but don't write long sentences and use long words for the sake of it: use them when appropriate and relevant. There's a pattern to good writing, which one could characterise as 'three-one-three', or 'five-two-five' or something similar. By this I mean, write three long sentences, then one short one, then three long ones. Or, five long, two short, then five long, and so on. Sometimes you can reverse the pattern, and write three short, one long, three short, for example. The main thing is to mix them.

### Choice of words

If you intend using unusual words to spruce up your writing, do so sparingly, and do ensure that you use them correctly. Don't rely on a thesaurus; a thesaurus will tell you all possible synonyms for a word, but won't necessarily explain that you can only use some of them in certain contexts. You can make some amusing or even shocking errors if you aren't careful. For example, let's imagine I want to write this:

> The human memory is a complicated system that depends on a range of processes to do its job.

Now imagine I decided that I wanted to make it sound clever, so I used my word-processing software's thesaurus and chose words to change without knowing exactly what was right and wrong. This is what could happen:

> The human recall is a convoluted organism that depends on a series of processes to do its occupation.

I've read sentences like this, and worse, and it is clear that the student has simply relied on a thesaurus. This just feels uncomfortable to the reader. Sadly, there's no substitution for reading, from which you learn how words are and aren't used, and then you can apply them yourself. Practice does make perfect – or closer to it.

### Spelling, grammar and punctuation

Grammar and punctuation is perhaps the hardest of all to put right quickly. From time to time you'll come across people who claim that grammar and punctuation aren't really important. They are trying to be sensitive, perhaps. Either that, or they are plain misguided. Fundamentally, your use of language *does* matter – it's just that it doesn't matter more than anything else on earth. It's not the biggest issue facing humankind, but to say that it doesn't matter is off the mark. People in positions of power, including those with the power to give you a job or turn you away, can usually write well, and they will judge you if you can't: the world is like that. This is not just about prejudice; in fact, writing clearly means writing well, and that means putting commas in the right places, knowing the difference between a colon and a semicolon, understanding apostrophes and so on. They really do make a difference. Think about how difficult it would be to read a textbook if the author and publisher hadn't bothered to check such things. Recently, the Chilean mint fired employees who failed to spot that the 2008 50 peso coin was printed and circulated with 'REPUBLICA DE CHIIE' printed on it.

If someone tells you that spelling and grammar don't matter, they haven't thought about it properly. My apologies if you suffer from dyslexia and you are reading this, because the mistakes you make are perfectly understandable and there's a limit to what you can do to change that, but, regardless of that, it *does* still matter, because if you get the spelling and grammar wrong you can end up saying something different from what you intended to say.

Let's start with spelling mistakes. Some spelling errors are funny. If you are making a serious point, you really don't want make the reader laugh. Here are some examples I have come across:

- The participants were told to wait for ten minuets.
- Standardised insurrections were used.
- Participants were given a short massage.
- The questionnaire was designed to gather information on how much wine, beef and spirits people drank in the average week.

- The distraction task involved a puzzle and those taking part had to put various pants in order.

These types of error often occur through the use of spelling checkers. Word processing software has no idea what you mean to say and simply finds a word close to the one you've misspelled. This is sometimes referred to as the *Cupertino effect*, and the software that produces the effect is sometimes called a *spilling chucker*.

On the subject of amusing errors, some mistakes can lose you money and even put you out of business. Imagine a menu where on offer were 'crapcakes', 'sweat and sour chicken' and 'fried squit'. One letter in each case is wrong, but when you are selling people food you really don't want to make them think about unpleasant things.

Often the errors aren't funny, but confuse a literate reader. If you confuse your reader, or slow down their reading, you could create a bad impression. For example:

- Save Are Jobs!
- We asked for the participants' name.

The second of these is very confusing if you know how to use possessive apostrophes properly. The sentence as it stands says that there are multiple participants (because the apostrophe is outside the plural), but 'name' is singular. So, what this actually means is that there were multiple participants with one name between them. This is probably not what the writer intended, but the reader has to stop and think before they can continue. If the sentence was correct from the outset, they could simply have read without interruption of flow.

This isn't a book on grammar, but it is important to reiterate the key point: clear English genuinely helps a document come across better, and that will increase your marks.

### First person versus third person

Another common problem of style is excessive use of the first person. You might have wondered why you are generally told to avoid writing 'I think . . .', 'In my opinion . . .', and so on, and instead are encouraged to write 'One could argue that . . .', 'It could be said that . . .' and so on. It's not because your lecturers are old-fashioned and stuffy: there are two key reasons. The first is that if you use the first rather than the third person constantly, you end up with an essay that reads as if you are showing off: 'me, me, me, me, me'. No one likes to hear someone going on and on about what they think, so why would you have an essay full of 'I' this and 'I' that? Secondly, there are many more ways to say something in the third person than in the first person. This means that the essay reads better, because it isn't repetitive. You may never have thought about either of these things before, but hopefully you can now see why it's important to avoid the first person. It genuinely does help work read better.

Here's a table to show how much more expressive you can be in the third person:

| First person | Third person |
|---|---|
| I think . . . | One can argue that . . . |
| I think . . . | It can be argued that . . . |
| I think . . . | It might be said that . . . |
| I think . . . | One might think that . . . |
| I think . . . | There are those who would claim that . . . |
| I think . . . | It could be said that . . . |
| I think . . . | It would be reasonable to suggest that . . . |
| I think . . . | A fair interpretation would be that . . . |

However, the use of the first person isn't always wrong. In fact, in many qualitative research circles it is considered appropriate. Qualitative work often doesn't shy away from accepting the fact that our attempts to understand the world are opinion-based, and using the first person allows for that 'honesty', if you like. Some qualitative researchers claim that to pretend that the researcher is somehow dispassionate and distanced from the work not only tells a lie, but loses the value of the way in which the researcher is embedded in the research. This is by no means a universal opinion, and some qualitative researchers prefer to use the third person, but there is a growing number who use 'I' or 'we' as a matter of course.

My advice is to try to use the first person carefully and not to overdo it. Whatever your philosophical position, if you keep on writing 'I' this and 'I' that you will sound egotistical and your writing will become clumsy. Read some qualitative work that uses the first person and you will see what I mean by its careful use. Very often, the entire problem can be avoided. It's fine to say 'I' or 'we' now and then, but at other times use phrases like 'this author' or 'this researcher'. Look over your work, and check that you haven't become repetitive. No one wants to read sentence after sentence in a results section that says 'I think that' or 'in my opinion' over and over again, whether it's a qualitative piece or not.

## Answering the question

Students often lose valuable marks by wandering away from the point and failing to answer the question asked. Instead they often answer a related question, or one that has captured their attention and interest. A sure-fire way to get poor marks is to miss the point. There's an easy way to avoid this problem: identify what the question is about before you start writing, and keep referring back to it as you write. Pick out key words in the question and stick to them. If the question asks you to compare three theories, make sure you write about three, not two or four. This sounds obvious but it's a common mistake. If the question asks for evaluation, not description, don't use up half the space available setting the scene; get down to the business of evaluation as soon as possible. If you are asked to explain why a theory works, make sure that you concentrate on the crucial word, which is 'why'. The question isn't about whether the theory works, since that's already been assumed by the question's setter. They want you to assume it works too, and explain *why*.

Suppose your essay title is 'What is time?'. That sounds as if it is more likely to be a question for a physics student than a psychology student, or at least you'd think so. The classic descriptive answer would state that time was a way of measuring our progress, and that it was measured in seconds, hours, minutes and so on, and that these are based on astronomical phenomena like the time taken for the earth to turn around the sun. Unfortunately, that isn't an answer to the question at all; it's just a description of how to measure time, not what it is. A proper answer to the question is just as much about psychology as it is about physics. Does time even exist? Not all physicists are convinced that it does. It could be a perception, a psychological phenomenon. You can't touch time, and you can't (apparently) travel in it, unlike the other dimensions. I can go up and down and backwards and forwards, and from side to side, but I can't do that in time. I can't see time, I can't change time and I can't travel in time. A critical answer to the question would seriously wonder about time's very existence, given that there is no tangible evidence that it is real. I say that I can't travel in it, but this isn't quite true; I can, but only forwards. That makes it fundamentally different from the other dimensions. That's an example of critical thinking in action; tearing things apart and recognising what something is and what it isn't. Time is what we use to make sense of what already happened and what hasn't happened yet, as distinct from what is happening now. Beyond that, it is seemingly impossible to characterise it. However, this is a circular argument, because the terms 'already happened', 'hasn't happened yet' and 'happening now' are based upon the assumption of time's existence. However we approach this, we end up stumbling. An essay that recognises this, instead of simply talking about minutes and hours and days, is a critical essay.

## Lacking depth

You may have had feedback claiming that something you wrote lacked depth. It's a common criticism, and it's another way of saying that an essay is missing critical evaluation or analysis. A shallow essay just describes or states what other people have said, whereas a 'deeper' essay is one that contains some original ideas and weighs up the evidence on an issue.

Students often mistake long words and complicated sentences for depth. That isn't depth, but rather style. While a certain writing style and depth often are found together, they don't have to be, and if you feel that emulating an academic style and writing with depth is too much, favour depth as the thing to concentrate on. Never sacrifice depth to make the style suitably 'sophisticated'; you can hide a profound thought by covering it with fancy language. Save the eloquent turns of phrase for the shallow ideas, and present your deepest thoughts as simply as you can.

## Lacking structure or planning

Another common feedback comment is that your essay lacks structure, which amounts to the same thing as saying that it hasn't been planned properly. Very few people can produce a document that has all the right things in the right places without planning. Even successful writers usually spend time working out a structure, deciding what to say and when to say it. Many student essays feel like catalogues of facts on a subject. You may have been told to include lots of citations and back up your points with research studies, so there's a tendency to cram as many of those in as you can, to the detriment of any structure, pattern or even argument. Choosing your evidence carefully is much better than trying to list all of it.

Before starting your essay, identify what the question is asking, what the key words are, and think about how you will structure an argument on the subject. It's clear to me that many students haven't thought about what their argument should be. This is a crucial problem that can make the difference between low and high marks. What is your point? Have you got one? And, most important of all, if you have one, does it come across in the essay?

Most students write essays using a common, off-the-shelf structure that they have been taught and tend to adhere to. He said this, she said this, then they said this, and she did this, and he said this about what she said, and they said this, and he said this about that, and then he invented this, and she refined it, and he said this about it, and so on. That's a catalogue of facts. Given that all psychology is about behaviour, there is usually critical insight you can add to most essays that can shift your mark upwards. Find a way to answer the question 'What does that tell us about why we do things?' Often the literature on a subject fails to adequately address that question, and when it does, it misses the point. Surely the primary issue of psychological research is to find out why we do things? Often the literature explains *what* we do, not why. Or *how* we do it, but not why. Never, in your own essays, mistake 'how' for 'why'. The gap between 'how' and 'why' is another way of characterising the distance between descriptive and critical.

Additional tricks to improve structure include making sure that each paragraph has one new idea in it, that each paragraph flows from the last, and that the conclusion isn't just where you waste words repeating what you've already said. Read newspaper articles. They tend to be short and non-technical. Always look at the final paragraph carefully. The writer will be introducing a new point, right at the end. The final paragraph doesn't repeat the article at all. A conclusion is *not* a summary. In a good piece of writing, the author holds back a good idea to throw at the reader to create a final impression. Imagine a novel in which the last chapter just told you what had happened in the other chapters. You'd be fairly disappointed. Essays aren't novels, it is true, but most forms of writing have patterns in common. When you write something, you are writing for a reader. We all have characteristics in common that dictate what works and what doesn't in terms of entertaining and persuading us. So whether it is a novel, a newspaper article, a poem, an essay, or even a symphony, some structures work better than others. Ending on a distinctive note – it could be a high note or a low note, but it must be distinctive – is greatly preferable to ending blandly or simply repeating yourself. Save the best till last.

## Citing your sources

You are told to cite your sources, but when you do, you are told that your essay is like a catalogue of facts. This can feel as if you are stuck between a rock and a hard place. However, it's all about balance. It's wrong to make all sorts of points without explaining where they come from, but an undergraduate essay isn't meant to be a complete review of every piece of research ever performed on a subject.

Why do you have to cite your sources? If you are making a point that someone else has made, why do you have to cite them? The simplest answer is that if you don't, you are guilty of plagiarism, but that is like telling someone not to drive too fast because it's illegal. Why is it illegal? Plagiarism is a kind of theft, so it's morally questionable. However, there's another point which students often aren't aware of, but which is very important (and offers an exercise in critical thinking too): *how can you show people that you have some great ideas of your own?* How can you distinguish between things you've read and things you have thought? The answer is to cite the sources for ideas which aren't yours, leaving the uncited ideas and arguments as, by implication, your own. If you haven't placed a reference next to a point, the reader assumes that it has come straight from your own mind. That's why you are plagiarising if you don't put names next to ideas that aren't your own. How otherwise could I know the difference between your own ideas and someone else's that you didn't bother to credit?

This distinction is sometimes called *referential* versus *rational* justification for your arguments. 'Referential' means that you refer to other people's work to support your claims, while a 'rational' justification instead relies on the strength of the argument itself, and on logic. If you don't cite work, the reader implicitly assumes you are providing a rational argument, not a referential one. When you provide a referential argument but pass it off as a rational one, you've plagiarised.

## Learning for thinking

This means structuring your learning so that it is conducive to critical thinking. Ideally what you want to achieve is the style of thinking of an expert in a subject. What is it about an expert that makes them different from a novice in the way that they think about things? They tend to think about disparate pieces of information in a way that stresses interconnectedness. They can see links where other people see individual items. The mind of an expert isn't just full of 'stuff'; just knowing a lot doesn't make you an expert. What makes you an expert is having multiple paths that allow you to access information. The more you have thought about something, the more you have ways of digging that information out of your mind from various angles.

Let us take an example. Here are some facts that we can try to learn.

- If you count the seconds since the universe is thought to have begun, that number is much, much smaller than the possible ways of ordering the playing cards in a pack.

- J. J. Thomson won the Nobel Prize for discovering the electron, a particle. His son, G. P. Thomson, won the Nobel Prize for discovering that the electron could be conceptualised as a wave.

- One of the largest numbers we can possibly conceive of and use is Graham's number. It is so large that we cannot possibly know what it is, nor ever write it down, but we know it ends in 7.

- Things that happen now can affect what happened in the past, according to quantum mechanics.

- Heisenberg's Uncertainty principle states that you can know where a particle is, or its velocity, but not both at once.

- If time travel is possible, you can't travel backwards in time from the moment you invent the machine to do it. You have to wait a bit, because you can't travel to a time earlier than the machine in which you are travelling was created.

Trying to learn these things can be quite difficult for the average person for a number of reasons. One is that they don't necessarily make sense, superficially anyway. At least some of seem very counter-intuitive, so fitting them into a mental model that is coherent is difficult unless you really understand them. Another reason is that they are essentially, to most of us, unrelated facts. However, to someone with knowledge of mathematics and quantum mechanics, they fit together quite nicely. The work of the father and son Thomsons directly feeds into the nature of retrospective causation (things that happen in the present or future affecting the past), since it is the experiments that show the duality of the electron as a wave or particle that also show this kind of strange backwards time effect. These map onto the fact about time travel, which also maps onto Heisenberg's Uncertainty principle, which is about the nature of the electron as a particle with specific properties and measurable versus immeasurable characteristics. If you understand the mathematics behind quantum mechanics, the nature of Graham's number (and why you might need it) and the calculation of the number of seconds since the universe began are all meaningful to you. To most of us, however, these are just unconnected statements, but learning a list of facts like this is easy for a physicist.

An expert therefore makes many mental associations. The expert sees connections, and can also create connections where they are less than obvious. Because of the mental networks they create, they can take on more and more information, assimilating it, learning new things quickly and being able to construct all sorts of interesting arguments because of the knowledge they can use to weave them. Now here's the important point. An expert recognises another expert. Therefore, if you can create arguments that an expert would make, by pulling together all sorts of facts to show that you possess your own mental network of understanding, you'll look like an expert too, and you will be given credit for it in your work. That's the difference between a mundane essay and a first-class one.

---

## CHAPTER 5 – CRITICAL QUESTIONS

1. Now that you've read this far in the book, you should be able to apply critical insights to allow you to mark your own work effectively. Take a piece of work you did a long time ago, and mark it as if you were the lecturer. Practise giving useful feedback.

2. There are plenty of essays scattered around the internet. Try printing some and 'playing' at being their marker.

# 6   Getting Fit for Critical Thinking

## FOSTERING A CRITICAL MINDSET

Everything we have discussed so far hinges on a particular mindset that, if you develop it, means that you naturally think critically about everything. That is not a bad thing, even if it can occasionally spoil your fun when watching a mindless movie. There are two things that you need to practise if you are to develop the critical mindset: *externality* and *mindfulness*. They are connected concepts, but are almost opposites.

### A sense of externality

By 'externality' I mean the ability to see things as another would see them. It means walking in someone else's shoes, assuming a perspective outside of your own and thinking about what the world looks like from a different angle.

This is as important a skill for psychologists as for other scientists, because you need it when writing reports. Far too often students leave crucial detail out of research reports because they have failed to imagine what a naive reader would make of what they have written. If you can imagine what another person would think when reading your work, your work instantly improves.

Thinking about the perspectives of others is also useful in helping you to avoid ethnocentricity – assuming that just because you think or feel something, it is likely to be what other human beings think or feel. It is true that we all have a lot in common, but it's a step too far to assume that we have *everything* in common. What seems easy to you may be very difficult for someone else, and vice versa. What seems like common sense to you may seem weird to someone else; there's no right or wrong, just differences of opinion or of culture.

One of the best ways to develop a sense of externality is to listen to others. You'd be surprised how often you don't, even when you think you do. Make a conscious effort to listen and you'll be amazed how much more you learn. Another important way to develop critical thinking is to seek out new experiences. How often do you do the same old things in the same old way? If you're honest, you probably eat the same foods most of the time, visit the same places, watch the same kind of films and TV and read the same books. You listen to the same radio shows and you go to bed at about the same time. You speak to the same people over and over, and you probably, as a result of it all, think the same things over and over again. There is a way to change this. It's good to experience new things, to break your routine sometimes, and it helps your mind to develop. The saying that 'travel broadens the mind' is an example. If you don't have much money, walk somewhere you haven't walked before. If you can't walk, look somewhere new, and so on. There's always something different you can do. Do it, and think about it while you are doing it and afterwards. Many of the things you take for granted may start to seem strange when you look at them from a different angle.

Something to try is a *day of difference*. Set your alarm clock for a time you don't normally get up. If you normally brush your teeth before washing, reverse it. Try something new for breakfast. Take a different route to work or university, and sit in different places from those you typically sit in and so on. There are hundreds of ways in which, in a single day, you can change your routine. See how it makes you feel. Unless you are someone who becomes upset when routines are broken, it will make a positive difference to you. It is the basis of a lot of advice on how to increase your well-being. On a larger scale, look for opportunities to do new things, and perhaps once a month try something new to you. It doesn't matter if you don't enjoy it; the very act of doing something novel will help you to get a new perspective on life, which will improve your critical thinking skills. You will start to question the things you usually do. Every time I travel somewhere it makes me realise that there are a thousand ways to do things, and none of them are the 'best' way. Diversity is what makes things interesting. Recognition of diversity and opinion is what helps us to understand ourselves and others better.

**TRY SOMETHING NEW
FROM TIME TO TIME**

## *Mindfulness*

Mindfulness is a very important concept in the world of Eastern mysticism, and is of growing usefulness in a range of therapeutic interventions. In contrast with a sense or externality or 'otherness', mindfulness involves being vigilant and especially aware of oneself and one's surroundings. It involves developing a view that concentrates your mind on the very things that you normally take for granted.

Mindfulness is also very cheap to practice; it costs nothing. Right now you are reading this book. Look at the page – *really* look at it. Think about what it is. It's a piece of paper. That paper is made from trees. You have no idea where those trees came from. Nor do I, even though you are reading my words. In fact, you are reading this some time after I wrote it. You have no idea how I feel as I write this, or what room I am sitting in, or what my chair is like, or what kind of computer I have, or what I can see if I look to my left. I don't know where you are reading this, or what you are like. I don't know how old you are, or even what sex you are. I don't know if you were born in Auckland, New Zealand, Minneapolis USA or Wakefield UK. But right now there is a connection between us, in that I am writing this and you are reading it, despite the fact that I am writing in the present, and you are reading in the present, but the two presents are different times. All that deep thinking can arise merely from glancing at the page; you have become mindful of something that was always there, but you didn't reflect on it before. Now you have.

Mindfulness is often used as a form of meditation, in which you are required to concentrate on something you normally take for granted, like your own bodily sensations, breathing for example. You focus on these things in order to have an increased awareness. Positive psychology approaches take mindfulness a step further, in asking that you become interested or grateful for the things you normally don't even think about. In some ways, mindfulness is like looking through a microscope at your life.

A balanced combination of externality and mindfulness gives you precisely the thinking skills you need to impress people with your critical views. Being hyperaware of yourself, and the effects of what you do and say, while being cognisant of the views and perspectives of others, is a perfect balance between the inner world and the outer world. To put it bluntly, if you can get these two things right, then you've got critical thinking covered. Being able to look at things from two different perspectives, the microscope and the telescope, if you like, is the sign of a person with a developed set of critical thinking skills.

# CRITICAL READING

If you are going to make the most of what you read, you need to read critically. That may sound obvious, but many people don't read critically. You've got to remember that the writer's job is to present a convincing argument, using all the tricks of the trade to make you agree with them along the way, so that at the end they've persuaded you that they are right. Critical reading is about resisting being seduced, maintaining a more neutral stance throughout the argument and questioning points made along the way.

The first thing to shake off is the assumption that published words are unquestionable. Writing a book is not an exact science, and the principles of sciences really don't apply. It is true that most publishers won't let you say something outrageous, but beyond that there really aren't many rules. Journal articles are much more rigorous, in that they are subject to editorial processes and peer review, but that just means getting your research past three people. If those three people share your opinions on a subject, getting through isn't always the struggle you'd imagine, even if the research is flawed. You need to show some respect for the process, and you can't just assume that everything you read is rubbish and lies and valueless. Most things you read will be well written, well researched and worth *something*. Critical reading is about working out what that 'something' is.

A common trick used by writers is to say 'Let us assume that . . .' In common language, they might say 'Bear with me on this . . .' They then make an assumption which is dubious, and the rest of a long, complicated argument holds up only if the original assumption is true. However, because they asked you to bear with them, you did so, and forgot later that everything was based on a faulty premise. Look out for arguments of this type early on in what you read. Authors often build grand theories on the shakiest of foundations and get away with it because you agreed to bear with them. For example, imagine a theory built on the assumption that people are fundamentally cruel. The writer states this and then goes on to explain how this basic human cruelty works its way into every aspect of human endeavour, with layer upon layer of examples. What doesn't change is that the idea that people are fundamentally cruel is an *assumption*, not a fact. Freud's work is based on an assumption that we have a subconscious mental life. If that isn't true, Freud hasn't got much to go on. Generally arguments fall into one of three camps: they are based on fact, theory or faith. When reading critically, you must identify which arguments belong in which camp, because the conclusions you draw will need to be grounded in this analysis. Arguments based on faith are the least useful from a critical point of view, but look out for arguments based on faith that are disguised as arguments based on theory. Also, keep your eyes open for arguments based on theory presented to you as those based on fact. Only arguments based on fact are 'safe' – and even those could be based on dubious facts.

Critical reading isn't a million miles away from social construction-ism and critical psychology. In critical psychology we are taught to identify assumptions and question them, and in social constructionism we are faced with the possibility that everything is a social construc-tion, and that our attempts to understand the world are attempts at deconstructing the narratives that make us what we are. Our very exis-tence is made up of our descriptions of our existence, so we'd better have a good look at those descriptions. That is what these branches of philosophy and psychology are about; if you study critical psychology, you will be well placed to read and write critically yourself. Conversely, learning about critical thinking will also help you to understand what critical psychologists and social constructionists are talking about.

One thing to remember is that the author's credentials can reveal a lot about the arguments made. This is not to suggest that a biologist can't make good points about politics, or that a politician can't have insights into human behaviour, for example, but generally speaking people should stick to pronouncing on areas in which they are quali-fied. By investigating the background of a writer, you will understand their arguments better. Unfortunately, psychology is one of those subjects in which, despite the long training required to become a psy-chologist, everyone thinks they can write or proclaim about human behaviour. The danger here is that a lack of training can mean that the writer or presenter doesn't really know everything they need to know to be able to construct a sensible argument. You would not go to a car mechanic for advice on your diet. You would not go to a doctor for help with a crossword puzzle. You would not ask an archaeologist how to fit a boiler. So, why is it that so many non-psychologists theorise and write about human behaviour?

Look out for disguised psychology, too. There is currently a great deal of interest in the application of economic theory to issues outside economics, such as human behaviour and other unusual subjects. If you've ever read any of the books on this subject, one thing should strike you: the authors aren't writing about economics *per se* at all. Many such books, written by economists, are actually books about psychology and game theory. So, these are economists writing almost entirely about psychology and biology. The conclusion that economics is (a) fascinating and (b) tells us a lot about the human world doesn't hold water, because the theories, examples and critical insights being employed aren't really from economics. I know you hate carrots, but I give you peas, tell you they are carrots, and now you love carrots. No?

You'd be forgiven for thinking that critical reading is all about finding out what is *wrong* with something you're reading. That really is only half the story. It is true that you are trying to catch the writer out, but just as resolutely you are hoping to find things in their writing that are well grounded, help to support theories and are difficult to argue against. Critical reading is about spotting the wheat, not just poking about amongst the chaff. In fact, you are only really interested in the chaff because it is something you have to accept in order to get to the wheat.

If you can read critically, you ought to be able to summarise too. It's therefore worth pausing on that skill and testing yourself.

# SUMMARISING

Summarising, or creating a précis of another document, is a valuable skill, and shows that you can separate the wheat from the chaff. As for many things, the best way to summarise is to work from a checklist. A systematic approach is often the best way, and a checklist means that you don't forget things you need to do or consider. To summarise a piece that already exists, consider the following:

- Read the piece, and note how many paragraphs there are. This is often the number of key points you need to convey in the summarised version.
- Identify the key words in the arguments.
- Remove any descriptive words that are merely poetic or rhetorical but which don't add to the piece.
- Cut out any scene setting or introductory words, and any repetition or summarising the author has done.

Often you will be summarising something you've written yourself, in which case you needn't worry about having to paraphrase to avoid plagiarism; the commonest form of summary for a psychologist is writing the abstract for a research report. However, do everything you can to avoid plagiarism if you are summarising someone else's work.

Try summarising this:

One of the most fascinating and rewarding things about psychology is the fact that so many of the seemingly separate areas combine together in interesting ways. Rarely does one fail to see a link between areas if one looks hard enough. For example, developmental psychology itself doesn't mean anything unless you consider what exactly is being studied in terms of development. We have social development, cognitive development, language development and so on. Therefore, it is important to consider social psychology, cognitive psychology and psycholinguistics. If we decide to look at cognitive psychology, in particular memory, we end up studying memory of something. It might be memory of words, in which case psycholinguistics is relevant again, or of pictures or objects, in which case visual perception must be taken into account. Of course, even when we study visual perception, we cannot forget that every picture is a picture of something. That something is also a word, so we are back to language again. If we choose to study social psychology, then a lot hinges on memory, perception, language, and even elements of biological psychology underpin social behaviour, since some aspects of social behaviour might be argued to be instinctual, for example attempts to attract a mate, or to gain prowess and respect of others. Similarly, you can't really study development in isolation from biological psychology, since our biological development (brain cells and so on) determines a lot of what we do and how we behave. Our phenotype is, after all, an expression of our genotype. The links are possibly infinite. It does mean that a psychologist has a difficult job, because nothing can be picked apart without reference to context, but is also means that it's difficult to become bored looking at the human organism in all its complexity and glory.

This piece contains a lot of examples, so it should be easy to cut it down. The writer has made just one point in lots of ways. Technically, you could reduce this to a single medium-length sentence. You'd lose lots of the rhetoric, it is true, but summarising isn't about maintaining the poetic features of a text. It isn't like translation or interpretation. So, the text above could be condensed to this:

> Psychology is a discipline which features many interconnected areas of study, which adds to its interest value but can make it difficult to examine any single area in isolation; for example, it is difficult to study development without reference to cognition.

Can you see how I have used critical thinking to pare the original text down to the simplest possible elements and present those, and only those? I could even cut it down further:

> Most areas of psychology are interconnected, adding to its interest value, but making it difficult to examine one in isolation, such as development without reference to cognition.

I began with a piece of 300 words. I summarised it in 41, then cut that further to 27. I don't think I can bring that down further, but 27 is just 9 per cent of the original. I did this by reading the text, identifying

the crucial point, and writing that point in my own words while avoiding all the examples and distractions. It will surprise you to learn how often there are only one or two points in an entire piece of work. Whole books have been written which can be summarised in a single sentence. Naturally, a lot of the pleasure of reading is lost, but summaries are not for pleasure.

---

## CHAPTER 6 – CRITICAL QUESTIONS

1. Choose an article that is available in text form, preferably in a psychology journal. Many journal articles are accessible as text, especially if you are using your own library systems and your institution is a subscriber. Try summarising the article to half of its length, then try cutting that by half again. It might be very difficult, but it will be excellent practice for learning the tricks associated with saying things in fewer words.

2. As an exercise in mindfulness, try making a cup of tea or coffee, but pausing and thinking about every step in the process. Then exercise mindfulness when tasting the drink too. Once you've done that, read about tea ceremonies in Japan.

You've reached the end of the book, and I would hope that something has happened to the way that you think about things. If you are a student, I also really hope that this book will help you to achieve better marks in your work. If there's one thing that I implore you to do, it is to approach the world with *polite scepticism*. Everything you hear and see is probably a mixture of truth, lies and confusion. The role of the critical thinker is to work out the proportions of each. However, you must do this while assuming that the source isn't deliberately lying. That's where the 'polite' bit comes in. Treat others with respect, because most people deserve it, most of the time, even when they are arguing weakly. Find ways to challenge faulty thinking that do not make you unpopular and do not hurt feelings. Showing a lack of respect is the easiest way to get ignored. If you shout at someone, it doesn't matter how right you are: you look wrong because you are shouting. Keep calm and make your points clearly, respectfully and without a trace of antagonism in your tone. The same applies to writing. A measured approach, which makes you seem quite reasonable, will always win over a rant, almost irrespective of the content.

You might want to ask yourself if you believe in truth, and whether 'the truth will out' over time. If there is a truth, and eventually truth wins, you just need to take part in the debate and give things a little push. If you don't believe in truth, then your role in the great critical thinking project is to convince others using the power of your arguments. Science fiction writer Theodore Sturgeon once said 'Ninety per cent of everything is crud'. That includes books, music, TV, ideas, theories and so on. In my view, critical thinking is all about finding the 10 per cent and working with it. But never become arrogant. Remember that 'Sturgeon's revelation', as it is called, always applies. So, when you have found the 10 per cent – or think you have – don't forget that 90 per cent of that is also crud.

Critical thinkers keep on thinking. Critical thinking is the driving force behind great human achievements and will always be so. It is impossible to separate critical thinking from creative thinking. Use your imagination, then put your imagination to the test. Think outside the box, please, but then use the box to keep your thoughts from running away.

# Exercises in Critical Thinking

1.  Pick up a newspaper, or watch a TV panel debate, and make note of the fallacious arguments made. If possible, note what categories they fall into, and, if you can, try to spot the 'favourite' poor arguments made by particular speakers.

2.  Examine the arguments for and against the existence of the Tooth Fairy. Try to construct a set of controlled experiments that would assist in your collection of information on the subject and the evidence either way. What are the ways in which you could test the assertion that the Fairy turns up at night and replaces your tooth with money?

3.  The following is the text of Gordon Brown's first speech when asked to take up the post of Prime Minister. Apply what you know about critical thinking to it:

I have just accepted the invitation of Her Majesty The Queen to form a Government. This will be a new Government with new priorities and I have been privileged to have been granted the great opportunity to serve my country and at all times I will be strong in purpose, steadfast in will, resolute in action in the service of what matters to the British people, meeting the concerns and aspirations of our whole country. I grew up in the town that I now represent in Parliament. I went to the local school. I wouldn't be standing here without the opportunities that I received there and I want the best of chances for everyone. That is my mission, that if we can fulfil the potential and realise the talents of all our people then I am absolutely sure that Britain can be the great global success story of this century. As I have travelled round the country, and as I have listened I have learnt from the British people – and as Prime Minister I will continue to listen and learn from the British people – I have heard the need for change, change in our NHS, change in our schools, change with affordable housing, change to build trust in Government, change to protect and extend the British way of life. And this need for change cannot be met by the old politics. So I will reach out beyond narrow Party interests, I will build a government that uses all the talents, I will invite men and women of goodwill to contribute their energies in a new spirit of public service to make our nation what it can be. And I am convinced that there is no weakness in Britain today that cannot be overcome by the strengths of the British people. On this day I remember words that have stayed with me since my childhood and which matter a great deal to me today, my school motto: 'I will try my utmost'. This is my promise to all of the people of Britain and now let the work of change begin.

4. In the autobiography of the late and controversial psychologist Hans Eysenck, he writes 'I always felt that a scientist owes the world only one thing, and that is the truth as he sees it. If the truth contradicts deeply-held beliefs, that is too bad. Tact and diplomacy are fine in international relations, in politics, perhaps even in business; in science only one thing matters, and that is the facts.' Use your critical thinking skills to dissect this position.

# Checklist for Critical Thinking

Some claim that it is possible to provide a checklist to aid critical thinking, and this could prove a useful tool for students. After all, much of critical thinking is about verifying the truth or falsehood of propositions, spotting rhetorical devices that mask a poor argument, and so on. A critical analysis of any text will require a number of passes, because on each pass we can look for something different.

The National Council for Excellence in Critical Thinking (part of the Foundation for Critical Thinking) developed a checklist for creating a critique or a critical essay on a subject.

1. All reasoning has a purpose.
   - State your purpose clearly.
   - Distinguish your purpose from related purposes.
   - Check periodically to be sure you are still on target.
   - Choose significant and realistic purposes.
2. All reasoning is an attempt to figure something out, to settle some question, solve some problem.
   - State the question at issue clearly and precisely.
   - Express the question in several ways to clarify its meaning and scope.
   - Break the question into sub-questions.
   - Distinguish questions that have definitive answers from those that are a matter of opinion and from those that require consideration of multiple viewpoints.
3. All reasoning is based on assumptions (beliefs you take for granted).

- Clearly identify your assumptions and determine whether they are justifiable.
- Consider how your assumptions are shaping your point of view.

4. All reasoning is done from some point of view.
   - Identify your point of view.
   - Seek other points of view and identify their strengths and weaknesses.
   - Strive to be fair-minded in evaluating all points of view.

5. All reasoning is based on data, information and evidence.
   - Restrict your claims to those supported by the data you have.
   - Search for information that opposes your position as well as information that supports it.
   - Make sure that all information used is clear, accurate and relevant to the question at issue.
   - Make sure you have gathered sufficient information.

6. All reasoning is expressed through, and shaped by, concepts and ideas.
   - Identify key concepts and explain them clearly.
   - Consider alternative concepts or alternative definitions of concepts.
   - Make sure you are using concepts with care and precision.

7. All reasoning contains inferences or interpretations by which we draw conclusions and give meaning to data.
   - Infer only what the evidence implies.
   - Check inferences for their consistency with each other.
   - Identify assumptions that lead you to your inferences.

8. All reasoning leads somewhere or has implications and consequences.
   - Trace the implications and consequences that follow from your reasoning.
   - Search for negative as well as positive implications.
   - Consider all possible consequences.

# YOUR OWN CHECKLIST

Why not try constructing your own critical thinking checklist that would be more specific to psychology, for example? What sorts of things should you include? When you've constructed it, test it over time and add to it by using it to construct and check your own arguments in essays and reports. In the course of your studies, it will grow into a very useful tool.

**argumentum ad hominem** a form of fallacy that attacks the source of an argument by making reference to flaws in that source which are not relevant to the argument in hand, such as when a lawyer tries to discredit a rape victim by claiming that they are sexually promiscuous.

**apophenia** the tendency for people to see meaning in random events that appear tied together, leading to the formation of conspiracy theories, for example.

**appeal to questionable authority** using an authority or expertise figure to strengthen an argument when their expertise or authority should not be taken for granted.

**argument** in philosophy, a series of statements building to a conclusion. It is contrasted with a 'disagreement'. It does not have to involve any more than one person, and can be entirely calm.

**argument from ignorance** the assumption that unless something has been proved to be false, it must be true.

**begging the question** an argument in which the conclusion is somehow inserted into the argument and is then used to substantiate the argument.

**clustering illusion** an illusion in which things that cluster randomly are assumed to be meaningful rather than random.

**domino effect** a situation in which a series of events are linked, each causing the other in sequence.

**false binary opposition** posing a choice as an 'either-or' when it is not necessarily the case.

**gambler's fallacy** a view, often held by gamblers, that in time their luck will change for the better if they keep on betting.

**hyperbole** repeating an idea unnecessarily, such as 'kneeling down', or 'round sphere'.

**Markov chain** a chain of events with known, separate probabilities linking those events. There is a known probability that A will lead to B, then a separate probability that B will lead to C, but A is not related to C at all. Thus the current step is dependent only on the previous one, but nothing before that.

**non sequitur**  an argument in which what is proposed does not follow from its premises. That is, there is a gap in logic between the start and end points of the argument.

**Occam's Razor**  the concept that the simplest explanation of something is to be preferred over more complicated ones unless proved wrong.

**pareidolia**  the brain's tendency to find patterns in visual or auditory noise where nothing meaningful is present, for example seeing faces in tree bark or clouds.

**post hoc ergo propter hoc**  the argument that, because two things happen together, one causes the other.

**premise**  the starting point of an argument. Usually, there are a series of premises, leading to a conclusion.

**propositional logic**  a branch of philosophy and mathematics concerned with the relationship between propositions and conclusions; that is, working out if something follows from what has previously been said. It has nothing to do with logic as we commonly use the word to imply 'truth'.

**protoscience**  'early' science, which is currently seen as opinion or pseudoscience, but which in time could become genuine science.

**pseudoscience**  something that has the appearance and characteristics of science to a lay interpreter, but is in fact not based in scientific thinking or evidence at all.

**rhetoric**  the art of using language well to persuade others. It relies on rhetorical devices, which are types of phrasing known to have an effect on the listener, such as repetition, assonance and alliteration.

**shifting the burden of proof**  this involves turning the concept of proof on its head and making a claim, but asking the other person to prove it isn't true.

**slippery slope**  an attempt to strengthen an argument, convince or persuade using the fallacy that if you accept A, then B will happen, and it will get worse, causing C and D and so on.

**snowball effect**  a phenomenon in which a small thing, for example an idea or a fashion, grows into something more important or serious.

**Socratic questioning**  a series of questions, popularised by Socrates, used to develop knowledge and to structure interrogation. They include questions of clarification, questions to probe assumptions, questions about points of view, questions about evidence, questions about implications and consequences, and questions about the question.

**special pleading**  arguing that everything must be a certain way, but with an exception that suits the argument. An example would be to say that everyone must obey the rules, except the leader. Unless there is a good, clear reason, this is not a valid argument.

**straw person**   an argument involving exaggerating or distorting the opposite opinion, thus making it easier to attack or discredit.

**Texas sharpshooter fallacy**   an analogy for what happens when we fit facts to our hypothesis, rather than beginning with a hypothesis and testing it afterwards.

**tu quoque**   if someone accuses you of something, suggesting that they have done the same thing themselves.

Adut, A. (2008). *On Scandal: Moral Disturbances in Society, Politics, and Art.* Cambridge: Cambridge University Press.

Browne, M. N. & Keeley, S. M. (2007). *Asking the Right Questions: a Guide to Critical Thinking*, Eighth Edition. New Jersey: Pearson/Prentice Hall.

De La Hunty, A. & Ashwell, M. (2007). Are people who regularly eat breakfast cereals slimmer than those who don't? A systematic review of the evidence. *Nutrition Bulletin, 32*, 118–128.

Dewey, J. (1909). *How We Think.* Boston: D. C. Heath.

Grice, P. (1989). *Studies in the Way of Words.* Cambridge, MA: Harvard University Press.

Paul, R., Fisher, A. & Nosich, G. (1993). *Workshop on Critical Thinking Strategies.* Sonoma State University, CA: Foundation for Critical Thinking.

Redelmeier, D. A. & Tversky, A. (1996). On the belief that arthritis pain is related to the weather. *Proceedings of the National Academy of Sciences USA, 93*, 2895–2896.

Shermer, M. (2008). Patternicity: Finding meaningful patterns in meaningless noise: Why the brain believes something is real when it is not. *Scientific American, 299*(6), 48.

Teigen, K. H. (1986). Old truths or fresh insights? A study of students' evaluations of proverbs. *British Journal of Social Psychology, 25*, 43–49.

Tversky, A. & Kahneman, D. (1974). Judgments under uncertainty: Heuristics and biases. *Science, 185*, 1124–1131.

van Wersch, A., Forshaw, M. & Cartwright, T. (2009). *Complementary Medicine and Health Psychology.* Maidenhead: Open University/McGraw-Hill.

The foremost repository for articles on critical thinking, including information for teachers, is to be found at the website of the Foundation for Critical Thinking.

For an extensive list of fallacies with examples, see also the Fallacy Zoo.

Browne, M. N. & Keeley, S. M. (2007). *Asking the Right Questions: a Guide to Critical Thinking,* Eighth Edition. New Jersey: Pearson/Prentice Hall.

Cottrell, C. (2005). *Critical Thinking Skills: Developing Effective Analysis and Argument*. Basingstoke: Palgrave Macmillan.

Fisher, A. (2001). *Critical Thinking: An Introduction*. Cambridge: Cambridge University Press.